D1543300

The Land and People of
CAMBODIA

The Land and People of ®
CAMBODIA

by David P. Chandler

HarperCollins*Publishers*

Country maps by Joe LeMonnier

Every effort has been made to locate the copyright holders
of all copyrighted materials and to secure the necessary
permission to reproduce them. In the event of any questions
arising as to their use, the publisher will be glad to make
necessary changes in future printings and editions.

The map on page 78 originally appeared in D.G.E. Hall's
Atlas of Southeast Asia (Macmillan Publishers Ltd., London).

The map on page 27 was redrawn with permission of
Macmillan Publishing Company from *Atlas of Southeast Asia*
by Richard Ulack and Gyula Pauer. Copyright © 1988 by
Macmillan Publishing Company, a Division of Macmillan, Inc.

THE LAND AND PEOPLE OF
is a registered trademark of
HarperCollins Publishers.

Library of Congress Cataloging-in-Publication Data
Chandler, David P.
  The land and people of Cambodia / by David Chandler.
    p.   cm.—(Portraits of the nations)
  Includes bibliographical references.
  Filmography: p.
  Discography: p.
  Summary: Introduces the history, geography, people, culture,
government, and economy of Cambodia.
  ISBN 0-06-021129-6. — ISBN 0-06-021130-X (lib. bdg.)
  1. Cambodia—Juvenile literature.   [1. Cambodia.]
I. Title.   II. Series.
DS554.3.C45   1991   90-5907
959.6—dc20   CIP
                                                               AC

10   9   8   7   6   5   4   3   2   1
First Edition

ACKNOWLEDGMENTS

I'm grateful to several people, whose names appear in the captions, for providing me with photographs. Two maps were originally drawn by Gary Swinton. The translations from the Vietnamese on pp. 96–7 are by Nguyen van Hung. Those from Khmer and French elsewhere in the book are my own.

I'm also grateful to Anne Blair for research assistance, and to my wife, Susan, as always, for her perceptive comments. My editor, Marc Aronson, and his assistant, Catharine Rigby, have been critical, assiduous, and supportive. The manuscript was also improved by the detailed comments of an anonymous reader. Many thanks to the indexer, Auralie Logan.

Everything I have written about Cambodia benefits from the insights of Cambodian friends, to whom I have dedicated this book. Among these men and women, I would like to single out Nar Keo, Chea Thon, and the villagers of Krol Ko hamlet (Kompong Speu).

Melbourne, Australia
David P. Chandler

Contents

THE WORLD

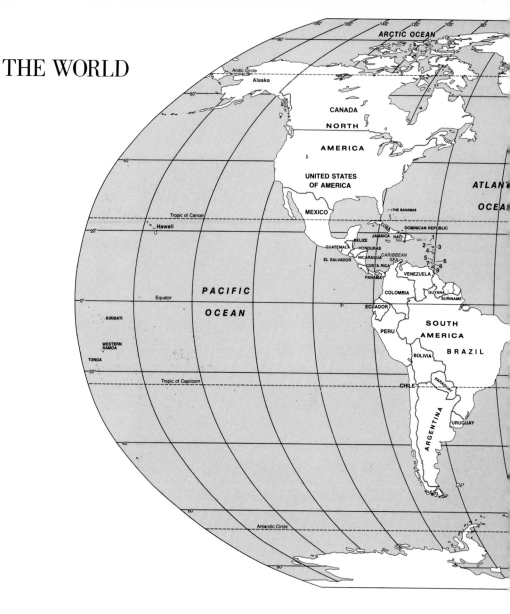

This world map is based on a projection developed by Arthur H. Robinson. The shape of each country and its size, relative to other countries, are more accurately expressed here than in previous maps. The map also gives equal importance to all of the continents, instead of placing North America at the center of the world. *Used by permission of the Foreign Policy Association.*

Legend

——— International boundaries

--------- Disputed or undefined boundaries

Projection: Robinson

```
0        1000      2000      3000 Miles
|———————|—————————|—————————|
0   1000  2000  3000 Kilometers
```

Caribbean Nations

1. Anguilla
2. St. Christopher and Nevis
3. Antigua and Barbuda
4. Dominica
5. St. Lucia
6. Barbados
7. St. Vincent
8. Grenada
9. Trinidad and Tobago

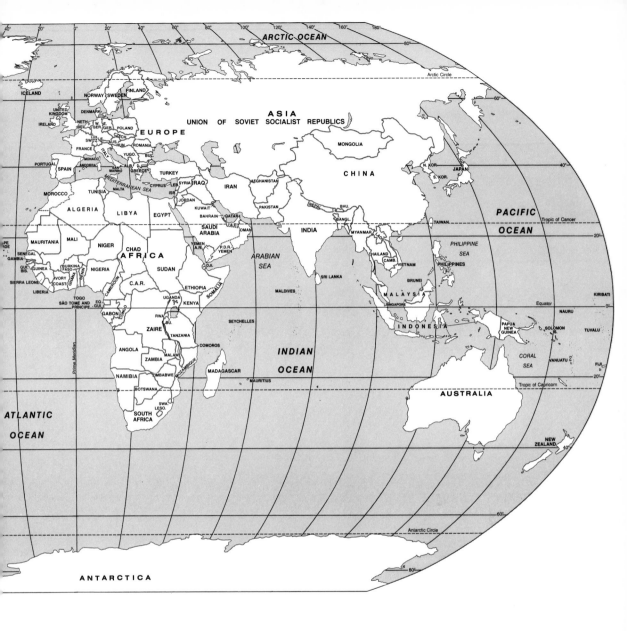

Abbreviations

ALB.	—Albania	C.A.R.	—Central African Republic	LEB.	—Lebanon
AUS.	—Austria	CZECH.	—Czechoslovakia	LESO.	—Lesotho
BANGL.	—Bangladesh	DJI.	—Djibouti	LIE.	—Liechtenstein
BEL.	—Belgium	E.GER.	—East Germany	LUX.	—Luxemburg
BHU.	—Bhutan	EQ. GUI.	—Equatorial Guinea	NETH.	—Netherlands
BU.	—Burundi	GUI. BIS.	—Guinea Bissau	N. KOR.	—North Korea
BUL.	—Bulgaria	HUN.	—Hungary	P.D.R.–YEMEN	—People's Democratic
CAMB.	—Cambodia	ISR.	--Israel		Republic of Yemen

RWA.	—Rwanda
S. KOR.	—South Korea
SWA.	—Swaziland
SWITZ.	—Switzerland
U.A.E.	—United Arab Emirates
W. GER.	—West Germany
YEMEN A.R.	—Yemen Arab Republic
YUGO.	—Yugoslavia

Mini Facts

OFFICIAL NAME: State of Cambodia

LOCATION: On the mainland of Asia, bounded on the east by Vietnam, on the north by Laos, on the west by Thailand, and on the south by the Gulf of Thailand

AREA: 68,898 square miles (181,035 square kilometers)—about the size of Missouri

CAPITAL: Phnom Penh

POPULATION: 7,300,000 (1990 estimate)

MAJOR LANGUAGE: Cambodian, or Khmer

RELIGION: Theravada Buddhism (c. 90 percent)

TYPE OF GOVERNMENT: Socialist republic

HEAD OF STATE: President

HEAD OF GOVERNMENT: President of Council (Prime Minister)

HEAD OF RULING PARTY: General Secretary

LEGISLATURE: National Assembly (5-year term)

ADULT LITERACY: 48 percent (1986)

LIFE EXPECTANCY: Males 45.3 years; females 48.2 years (1986)

PRINCIPAL PRODUCTS: Rice, rubber, corn, pepper, timber, fish, gemstones

CURRENCY: Riel

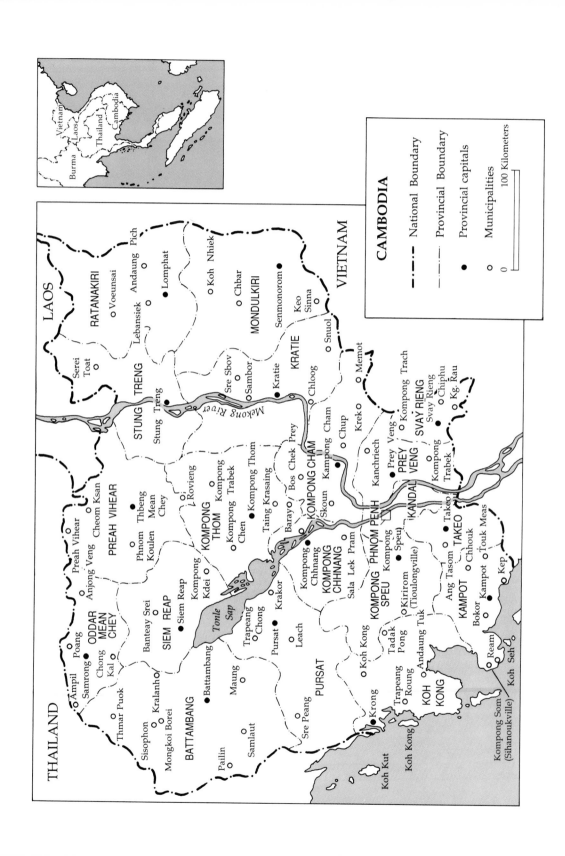

Starting from Zero

For nearly all adult Cambodians, April 17, 1975, was the last day of a war and the first day of a revolution. They remember April 17 as the day when their familiar world ended and a strange new Cambodia began.

For several days, the people in Phnom Penh, Cambodia's capital city, had known that the civil war, which had ravaged the country for five years, was almost over. The American Ambassador and his staff had been evacuated by helicopter on April 12. Two weeks earlier, Marshal Lon Nol, the chief of state, had been flown into exile. The city was cut off on all sides by rebel forces, the so-called "Red Khmers," or Khmer Rouge, who by then controlled the entire country, except for a few towns. On April 14, the Red Khmer forces began their final push against Phnom Penh.

The people in the city, over two million of them, were exhausted by the fighting. For months, rockets and artillery shells had fallen at random on the capital, killing and wounding men, women, children, and a few government soldiers. Food was running out. Electricity, water systems, and sanitation had broken down. Over a million people who had sought shelter in the city from the countryside were huddled in slums, under appalling conditions.

Everyone in Phnom Penh hoped that the end of the war would come soon and that it would bring Cambodians together to cooperate in rebuilding their country. Men and women who worked for the government, or had fought against the rebels, were willing to help. "I was ready to do anything," an electrical engineer has recalled. "The old society had been corrupt. There was so much suffering. I believed that with peace, everybody would work together, and conditions would improve."

Less fortunate people, unaccustomed to living in cities and in such poverty, longed to return to their villages and resume their lives as farmers or students. Government soldiers, many of them still in their early teens, were ready to lay down their arms.

These hopes and longings came to nothing. Over the next few days, the inhabitants of Cambodia's cities were driven out into the countryside. For the next four years, those who had been in cities and towns on April 17, 1975, were punished for "betraying" the revolution. They were called "new people" or "April 17 people," to differentiate them from the "old people" or "base people" who had lived in the countryside and supported the Red Khmers. The city dwellers were singled out for suspicion, mistreatment, and executions. They were put to work, along with everybody else, as farm laborers. Cambodia became a gigantic farm. Schools were closed, money and markets were abolished, and Buddhist monasteries were shut. The entire country was overturned.

Prisoners of war are beaten and pulled along by victorious soldiers. Bas-relief from Angkor Wat (eleventh century A.D.). Notice how some prisoners are being tossed by the elephant. The bas-relief is an eerie foreshadowing of the evacuation of Phnom Penh in 1975.
Walter Veit

The process lasted until the end of 1978. Over a million Cambodians, or *one person out of every seven,* died in this period from malnutrition, overwork, mistreated diseases, and executions. Many people have compared what happened to Cambodians at this time to the fate of European Jews under the Nazis in World War II. Some writers have used the word "genocide"—the killing of a race—to describe the Cambodian experience.

In 1970, Cambodia had been a peaceful, prosperous country, about to be plunged into a ruinous civil war. In 1975, the country was badly damaged. By 1979, when the revolution ended, it lay in ruins.

· 3 ·

April 17, 1975

None of these events could have been predicted by people in Phnom Penh on April 17, their thoughts were on their own survival and on the possibility of peace.

Cambodians get up before sunrise, to take advantage of the cool hours of the day. April 17 began early. People remember having breakfast with their families, and going off to work as usual, because there seemed no point in being frightened or alarmed by the prospect of the end of the war. It could come today or tomorrow.

No one knew much about the Red Khmers or thought they would be frightening. "They were Cambodians, after all, like us," a former student remembered. "We would understand each other, and know what needed to be done." After years of chaos, many were ready to accept orders from the Red Khmers. "Things had gotten so bad, with corruption, inflation, food shortages, and violence," a former teacher has said, "that we thought: 'If a revolution is necessary, that will be all right.'"

At 8:00 A.M., the government radio station, which had been broadcasting military music, went temporarily dead. By then, the city was jammed with new arrivals from the nearby countryside, the scene of the last battles. Many people returned home to await developments. Shopkeepers closed up. Others gathered in the streets "like birds released from their cages," as one of them wrote later, to welcome the Red Khmers. In residential areas, no traffic moved. The city, poised between war and peace, was eerily silent.

François Ponchaud, a French priest who had lived in Cambodia for many years, noticed the first rebel soldiers as they moved cautiously down the boulevard outside the Catholic cathedral, around 10 A.M.:

Small groups of young Khmers, hardly into their teens, began slowly moving into town. They were dressed in black, wearing black Chinese caps and Ho

Chi Minh sandals—soles cut out of old tires fastened to the feet with rubber thongs. Hung about them were Chinese grenades, antitank explosives, Chinese assault guns . . . They looked bewildered, on the verge of collapse, utterly remote from the people's jubilation.

None of the young soldiers replied when people spoke to them. They refused gifts of fruit or drinks of water. They wore no signs of rank. Many of them seemed never to have seen a city street before. They moved on, silently, along the major boulevards. By midday, the troops entering the city from different directions met. The war was over. They had won.

At noon, the last broadcast of the government, announcing that talks were being conducted with the Red Khmers, was cut off by a Red Khmer, who said, "We did not come here to talk. We enter Phnom Penh not for negotiation, but as conquerors." He repeated these sentences several times. After that, the radio went dead.

Evacuating the Cities

What happened next was completely unexpected. In the early afternoon, Red Khmers with loudspeakers began circulating in the city, in trucks, ordering everyone to leave immediately "for three days," claiming that "American planes are coming to bomb the city."

In some parts of Phnom Penh, people were not made to move out until the following day. By April 19, however, houses and shops and hospitals were empty, and a sea of people, hardly moving at all, filled the roads leading away from the capital.

Similar orders were issued in the remaining cities under government control. The largest of these was Battambang, in the northwest, which contained over 250,000 people at the end of the war.

On April 17, 18, and 19, over 2 million inhabitants of Phnom Penh walked away from the city. Those in the northern part of the city went north, those in the western part went west, and so on. Armed revolutionaries walked alongside, making sure that no one tried to escape. When asked for explanations, they gave none but referred to the *angkar padevat* (revolutionary organization), which, they said, "had to be obeyed." The Red Khmers were probably not aware that "revolutionary organization" was a name chosen by the Cambodian Communists to conceal their own existence.

For several days, people on some of the roads were packed together so tightly that they hardly moved. It took a week for them to reach the city limits. Along the way, many old people and little children collapsed and died from exhaustion, shock, and the overpowering heat. Clean water was hard to find, and food brought along from people's houses soon ran out.

Enduring the Revolution

Gradually, the crowds thinned out. The "April 17" people were allowed to settle in the country, where they were put to work growing rice and digging irrigation canals. Conditions were harsh; the revolution was the same everywhere. But newcomers fared somewhat better in the east and southwest of the country, which had been under Red Khmer control for several years. Little by little, the "revolutionary organization" took over every aspect of everyone's life.

The revolution overturned the past. A radio announcement not long after the liberation of Phnom Penh said that "two thousand years of Cambodian history have ended." The winners believed that a new era of independence had begun, when there would be "no exploiters and no exploited, no masters and no servants, no rich and no poor." When everyone was equal, it was thought, everyone would be happy.

Cambodians were being asked to start their lives from zero.

By the 1990's, some of the scars of the revolution had healed. Many remained. Nothing could make up for the terrible losses nearly everyone had endured. In some cases, only one or two people survived from families of ten or eleven.

But even after so much suffering, Cambodia was again menaced by civil war, this time between government forces—whose allies, the Vietnamese, had overthrown the Red Khmers in 1979—and the still-strong armies of the revolutionaries. The possibility that the Red Khmers might return to power frightened many Cambodians. Others were determined to fight, to prevent history from repeating itself.

The Land

Physical Characteristics

On a map, Cambodia looks like a walnut caught in the open jaws of its three large neighbors, Thailand, Laos, and Vietnam. On the fourth or open side, Cambodia faces the Gulf of Thailand, which is part of the South China Sea.

In Asia, where countries tend to be large (consider China, which covers 4.5 million square miles—11.7 square kilometers), Cambodia is relatively small, covering approximately 69,000 square miles (about 180,000 square kilometers). If it were an American state, it would be about the same size as Washington or Missouri.

Topographically, the country resembles a shallow dish. Forming the rim, two ranges of low mountains, the Cardamom and Elephant chains, follow the border with Thailand. In the northeast, the land rises to a plateau that is the beginning of another range of hills, the Annamite Cordillera, that forms a kind of backbone, running north to south, of Vietnam. These mountains and the plateau are heavily forested and have few roads or navigable streams. Not many people inhabit these regions, whose shortage of fresh water and prevalence of malaria make them hostile to human beings.

The rest of the country, or the inside of the dish, is a generally fertile plain that covers about half of the country, where perhaps nine out of ten Cambodians live.

The plain forms part of the basin of the Mekong, the world's tenth largest river, which flows for over two thousand miles from the mountains of western China into the South China Sea, near Ho Chi Minh City in southern Vietnam. For several hundred miles the Mekong passes through Cambodia. With its tributaries, the river provides water to irrigate Cambodia's fields, shelter for literally billions of fish, and a transportation route that is open the year round. Ships going between Phnom Penh and Ho Chi Minh City in Vietnam travel on the river. So do Cambodians who live in the villages and cities along its banks.

The Tonle Sap

The most important tributary of the Mekong in Cambodia is the Tonle Sap, sometimes called the Great Lake. The river flowing out of the lake bears the same name. The Tonle Sap is unusual for two reasons— because its flow changes direction twice a year and because the portion that forms a lake expands and shrinks dramatically with the seasons.

From November to May, Cambodia's dry season, the Tonle Sap drains into the Mekong at Phnom Penh. In June, however, when the year's heavy rains begin, the Tonle Sap backs up to form an enormous lake. Rain and snow much farther north along the Mekong also affect

Cambodia and Kampuchea

Since 1975, when the Pol Pot regime declared the spelling and pronunciation of their country's name in foreign languages to be Kampuchea, there has been some confusion about what the country should be called.

Cambodians, speaking their own language, pronounce their country's name as "Kampuchea," just as Danes refer to Denmark as "Danmark," Italians to "Italia," and so on. The Cambodian Communists asked others to pronounce the country's name their way while speaking foreign languages. They made no effort to pronounce the names of other countries in the way the people of those countries pronounced them, and even referred to some parts of the world, such as Latin America, in transliterated French.

The Vietnamese-sponsored People's Republic of Kampuchea continued this tradition, but broke with it in 1989, when the government changed its name to the State of Cambodia ("Ro't Kampuchea" in Khmer) and declared that the new name, in foreign languages, could be spelled and pronounced as before—that is, as "Cambodge" in French, "Cambodia" in English, and in other ways in other languages.

Because of this development, and because the name Cambodia is still more familiar to most readers in the West than "Kampuchea," "Cambodia" has been used in this book—except when the regimes calling themselves Kampuchea are mentioned.

Fish forms a major part of the Cambodian diet, and the Mekong River near Phnom Penh teems with fish. The nets are lowered into the water on flexible bamboo poles, a system perfected centuries ago.   Christine Drummond

this process. In November, when the rains diminish and the Mekong's flow subsides, the Tonle Sap drains back into it once again.

In the rainy season (June to November), this lake covers nearly a seventh of Cambodia's surface. However, by February, which is the driest month of the year, it has shrunk to a tenth of its maximum size. As it shrinks it leaves thousands of tons of fine mud behind every year, enriching the soil along its shores. By then, the Great Lake has also become the richest freshwater fishing ground in the world, yielding over a million pounds of fish for each square mile (half a million kilograms for 2.6 square kilometers) of its surface. During the rainy season, the floodwaters sweep up huge quantities of plants. As it grows smaller, the lake turns into a kind of vegetable soup, ideal for feeding fish.

Cambodia's Weather

In terms of weather, the Cambodian year breaks into two seasons—
rainy and dry, with the dry season itself composed of two parts—relatively cold and hot, in that order. The rainy season begins in June and
lasts until November. The "cold" season, at its height in December and
January, brings temperatures down to the the low sixties at night. In
these months, the rice harvest is gathered in throughout the country.
To most Americans and Europeans, these are the most pleasant times
to spend in Cambodia. Days are clear, breezy and dry; the temperature
hovers around 75 degrees Fahrenheit (24° centigrade), and travel by
road is neither dusty nor wet. Most Cambodians, however, find these
months chilly and unpleasant.

Gradually, in March and April, the weather gets hotter and damper.
Days and nights are sticky, airless, and uncomfortable, broken only by
a few light rainstorms. In many rural areas, the dryness means that
fresh, drinkable water is often hard to find, while stagnant water increases the likelihood of disease. The landscape, which had been bright
green at the start of the year, or golden where the rice fields have
matured, takes on a listless gray-brown color, as the harvested ricefields
bake and the soil cracks open in the relentless sunshine.

When the first rains come, in late April, the Cambodians begin their
Buddhist calendar and celebrate their New Year. As the rains intensify,
softening the soil, they ease the plowing and planting of rice and other
crops.

Everything grows quickly in Cambodia, and after a month of rain,
light at first, then gradually getting heavier, the landscape is green
again. Almost all of Cambodia's rainfall comes between June and November. During these months, the central plain gets nearly six feet (1.8
meters) of rain (compared with four feet *all year* in New York City and

less than two feet in Los Angeles). It never rains for very long, and seldom more than once a day. Instead, rain falls heavily for an hour or so, usually in the afternoon or evening, often to the sound of thunder. By October, most of Cambodia is completely soaked, and its ricefields and pastures are under a foot of water. Low-lying villages and city streets are often flooded, but the houses usually stay dry because most of them are raised off the ground by pillars or stilts.

These conditions are ideal for the cultivation of wet rice, but for centuries they have held back the development of overland communication. Even today, hundreds of Cambodia's villages are cut off from each other and from motorized traffic for several months of the year.

Cambodia's Resources

Cambodia's main resources are human and agricultural. The country has only small amounts of exploitable mineral wealth, but in the short term at least, as in Myanmar (the modern name for Burma), the exploitation of its forests could provide Cambodia with foreign income with which to modernize parts of its war-shattered economy. Similarly, the once-prosperous rubber plantations in eastern Cambodia might be restored, and rubber could regain its place among Cambodia's exports. Such developments will depend on the reestablishment of peaceful conditions in the country and on more widespread diplomatic recognition. In the meantime, rice is Cambodia's most important resource.

Rice

This grain has played a leading role in Cambodian life throughout the country's history. Under traditional Cambodian law, it was a crime to damage or even to insult a rice plant. Today, the Cambodian verb *sii*

While farmers in the foreground transplant rice seedlings from seedbeds to the fields where

baay (to eat) means literally "to eat rice," and nearly everyone eats rice two or three times a day. Perhaps as many as two thirds of the country's work force consists of rice farmers who grow food for themselves and their families and trade the surplus for other goods.

they will be harvested in several months, others plow the flooded fields with oxen.   Kelvin
Rowley

From the ninth to the fifteenth centuries A.D., a major kingdom
known today as "Angkor" flourished in Cambodia. Its wealth was based
on the systematic exploitation of rice. More recently, until war swept
through the country, rice made up more than half of Cambodia's ex-

ports, by value. Under the Red Khmer revolution, the government tried to triple rice production in order to earn foreign exchange to pay for industrial tools.

Since 1979, rice production has gradually risen, but by the early 1990's it had not yet reached pre-1970 levels, and Cambodia, once an exporter of 500,000 tons of rice per year, needed to import over 100,000 tons each year to feed its population.

Given the importance of rice, it is unfortunate that so much of Cambodia's population is crowded into those parts of the country whose soil is most poorly suited for agriculture—particularly the sandy regions south and southwest of Phnom Penh. The crowding means that for much of the twentieth century, many Cambodian farmers have coaxed their food from soils that should be cultivated less frequently, or not at all. Under these conditions, yields of rice are low—sometimes only 800 pounds (360 kilograms) of unhusked rice per acre. This is about half the corresponding figure for central Thailand, or even for northwestern Cambodia, areas that are traditionally referred to as the "rice basket" of Southeast Asia.

In the northwest, thanks to richer soils, more mechanization, and greater use of fertilizers, harvests in the rice-producing areas, particularly in Battambang province, can be twice as high as the national average. This was the area chosen by Pol Pot to take the lead in tripling national production. Unfortunately, the poor organization, hastiness, and city-based labor force thrown into the province meant that several hundred thousand Cambodians died of starvation, malaria, and overwork in the northwest alone between 1975 and 1979. Since 1979, the region has made something of a comeback, but progress has been impeded by shortages of livestock and machinery as well as by the presence of hostile guerrillas along the border with Thailand and in forested areas that might otherwise be opened up to cultivation.

Other Resources

Aside from rice, Cambodia's main agricultural resources are rubber, timber, and fish. Before the 1970's, Cambodia's rubber plantations covered over 200,000 acres (80,000 hectares), and sales of rubber abroad provided the Cambodian government with over $50 million a year in foreign exchange, equivalent to perhaps $200 million at today's prices. The rubber plantations were devastated in the war. Between 1979 and the late 1980's, new plantings were made, and by 1989 Cambodia was exporting some ten thousand tons of processed rubber. It will be many years before the country will be able to export larger quantities.

Cambodia's forests, which cover more than half of the country, have not been cut down because of shortages of modern equipment, the absence of logging roads, and the uncertainties resulting from nearly twenty years of war and isolation. In the late 1980's, timber along the Thai frontier was being logged and sold to Thailand without the knowledge or approval of central authorities. Logging practices still take little or no account of the impact of removing forest cover from the soil or of the future of regions whose timber has been logged. The environmental effects of uncontrolled logging, which has already devastated large parts of Africa, South America, and Southeast Asia, have not yet been felt in Cambodia. But the temptation of quick profits from cutting down apparently "useless" forests may be too great for some Cambodians to resist.

Cambodia's freshwater fisheries, another rich resource, have not yet developed into an export industry, except informally along the rivers to Vietnam. Progress has been slowed by wartime conditions and the prohibitively high investment that would be needed for boats, processing equipment, freezers, and canneries. Since 1970, Cambodia has been cut off from the kinds of foreign investment that might assist a fisheries program. As soon as peace is restored, developing such a program would be high on the agendas of many foreign countries, particularly Japan and Thailand. Both countries are also interested in harvesting Cambodia's timber. In the meantime, a lively trade exists between Cambodia and Vietnam in dried fish and in *prahoc* (fermented fish paste), used in both countries as a seasoning.

Other agricultural resources that were important before the 1970's, and could conceivably be revived, include cattle, pepper, corn, sugar, cotton batting, coffee, and jute. Tobacco and pineapples also have been grown in commercial quantities in the past. Like most of the countries of the region, Cambodia abounds in fruit—some of it familiar, such as oranges, bananas, grapefruit, and watermelon; and others less so, such as papaya, rambutan, and mangoes.

Cambodia's wild animals include elephants and tigers, which roam the forested northeast. Until recently there were rhinoceroses and wild oxen in this part of the country too. Brightly colored parrots, black and white ibises, kingfishers, and small, iridescent tropical birds are everywhere in the countryside. Domestic animals include chickens, pigs, and ducks, as well as water buffalo, used for plowing, and humpbacked cattle, used for plowing and pulling carts.

Cambodia's mineral resources, unlike its agricultural ones, are not particularly promising and remain to be developed. There are small deposits of iron and low-grade coal in Cambodia, as well as small quantities of phosphate and some gold in the riverbeds. Rubies and sapphires are mined along the Thai border, near Pailin. Petroleum deposits in the seabed of the Gulf of Thailand, largely claimed by Vietnam, still have not been developed, and at present Cambodia imports all its oil and gasoline.

Water, particularly in the Mekong, remains potentially an enormous

Coconut palm trees dot the Cambodian landscape. To harvest the sap, the owner ascends a makeshift ladder. Charles F. Keyes

resource for Cambodia. It could be harnessed, in the form of dams, to irrigate much of the central plain, to control periodic flooding, and to generate electric power not only in Cambodia but in neighboring countries as well. Unfortunately, wars and disagreements among the countries through which the Mekong flows have set back development of this resource, although a promising start was made, many years ago, under the auspices of the United Nations. These international initiatives may well be revived in the future.

Cambodia: Prosperous or Poor?

Cambodia, then, like so many other nations in the developing world, is an agricultural country, and, in terms of the cash incomes of its people, desperately poor.

In the past, Cambodia was able to earn foreign exchange to pay for imported goods by selling agricultural surpluses—of rice and corn, for example—or plantation crops, such as pepper, rubber, and cotton. Its normal patterns of trade were broken up in the wars of the 1970's. When the fighting died down, Cambodian trade became lively again, but more informal, which benefitted many individual traders but deprived the government of money it needed to pay for essential services, like electricity, schools, water, and highways. There was some question at the end of the 1980's if Cambodia would ever be able to trade its way back into the kind of prosperity that it had enjoyed in earlier times.

Of course, the word "prosperity" is a relative one. Even in the peaceful 1960's, Cambodia was one of the poorest countries in eastern Asia, at least in terms of individual income. It is hard for even a relatively poor Westerner to imagine just how poor—in terms of cash, choices about the future, and possessions—a Cambodian farmer or unskilled laborer has always been, or what an annual income of less than the equivalent of two hundred dollars means in terms of the everyday life of farmers and their families. In nearly all Cambodian families, everyone works hard to grow the food and earn the money needed to survive. Even so, by international standards most Cambodians are very poor.

Being poor in Cambodia means eating less than a pound of meat a month, and a family's earning less than six hundred dollars from a rice crop that has occupied most of its labor, intensively, for the equivalent of three months. For most Cambodians, there is little question of new clothes, gadgets, or vacations. The money from the rice crop has to last the farming family for an entire year, unless the husband leaves home to find another job—as a laborer in Phnom Penh, for example—or the wife manages to supplement their income by selling fruit, cloth, or cigarettes in the local market. Most Cambodians live below the poverty line and struggle hard to find enough food for themselves and their children. The difficulties are intensified because in the late 1980's a large proportion of the rural population—statistics are not precise, but perhaps as many as one in four—consists of families headed by women widowed in the wars of the 1970's and 1980's.

Women have always worked as hard as or harder than men in agricultural tasks, but usually alongside them, and today Cambodia suffers from a shortage of able-bodied men. Tens of thousands of other men are drawn away from productive work by service in the army and in labor battalions along the Thai–Cambodian frontier.

In some ways, of course, it's easier to be poor in Cambodia than in the West. First, there is the warm weather. Houses are not expensive to build, heating isn't needed, and people don't wear heavy clothes. In the second place, rice is cheap to buy, and for much of the year supplementary foods—fish, fruit, and vegetables—are easy to grow, catch, or barter. Third, the country is not yet overcrowded, at least in

Cambodians call plowing "waking the soil." The wooden plow, with an iron tip, is yoked to a pair of oxen. Similar plows are depicted in twelfth-century Cambodian sculptures. Kelvin Rowley

the east and the northwest, and there is still unoccupied fertile land that can be brought under cultivation.

If it is difficult for Cambodians to freeze or starve to death, it would be wrong for us to think of Cambodia as a tropical paradise. A Cambodian farmer, a widow living in Phnom Penh, or a day laborer usually has no savings or any valuable property. The state has almost no way to help them. In an emergency—an accident, a sudden illness, or a fire—death is much closer for such people than it would be for most North Americans, and the possibilities of their raising money, or receiving proper medical care, are much more remote. Hundreds of thousands of Cambodians live on the edge of survival, eking a bare living from the soil or from poorly paid casual labor. Most men and women in Phnom Penh have two or even three competing jobs. They are uncertain about the future and what it will bring for their children. This uncertainty, of course, has increased with the fighting and disorder of recent years.

In material terms, Cambodia, even with its agricultural resources and its potential for development, will probably always be very poor in

A woman irrigates her field by tipping water from a ditch into the field itself, surrounded by a low wall of earth.   Kelvin Rowley

A schoolchild on her way home near Kompong Speu. Notice the house built on stilts, and, left, the overloaded bicycle. Christine Drummond

comparison to countries like Japan, Canada, and the United States, or even to nearby countries like Thailand and Malaysia. It has two riches, however, that make it very interesting to study. These are its people and its history.

The People

Population Statistics

No definitive census has been taken in Cambodia since 1962, but most experts agree that by 1990 there were probably about 7.3 million people living in the country. Of these, perhaps one in ten, or 800,000, were in the capital, Phnom Penh. Because of wars, turmoil, and emigrations, the population of Cambodia today is about the same as it was in 1969. On the mainland of Southeast Asia, in recent times at least, Cambodia has always had the lowest population of any country except Laos.

The population is growing at a rate of about 3 percent a year, however, and this means that about 45 percent of the people are under the age of fifteen. These figures are high by Southeast Asian standards, but Cambodia is far from crowded. There is enough space and, potentially, enough food for many more people, but there are probably not enough jobs to make many Cambodians even moderately wealthy, and in the cities electricity, running water, and sanitation are in woefully short supply. In many rural areas they do not exist.

The Khmer

Cambodians, or Khmer (rhymes in Cambodian with "good-bye"), are overwhelmingly rural. Partly, this is a matter of preference; most Cambodians have always been farmers, and until the 1960's were reluctant to live in cities, where jobs were unfamiliar, food was more difficult to obtain, and living was expensive. Although urban life became more popular in the 1960's, all the cities were emptied by Pol Pot when he took power, and the two biggest ones, Phnom Penh and Battambang, now hold only 15 percent of the country's people. Similarly, many provincial cities, destroyed or abandoned in the war, have never recovered the populations they lost in the 1970's. Some of them, like Kompong Speu, have almost disappeared from the map.

Most Khmer have always lived in *phum* (small villages). The village is the basic unit of the Cambodian landscape and of Cambodia's social organization, despite attempts under Pol Pot to force hundreds of thousands of Cambodians to live in larger units, or communes. The cultivation of irrigated or flooded rice makes people join together to share the work of planting, transplanting, and harvesting the crop.

This work has always set the rhythm for Cambodian life. Under Pol Pot, people were made to work all year round, often on projects that provided few visible benefits, and where tens of thousands died from malnutrition, overwork, and executions. Scattered evidence suggests that after 1979, most rural Cambodians, in relatively secure areas at least, had formed themselves into units that resembled prewar villages, and resumed agricultural work aimed at providing food for the families who grew and collected it.

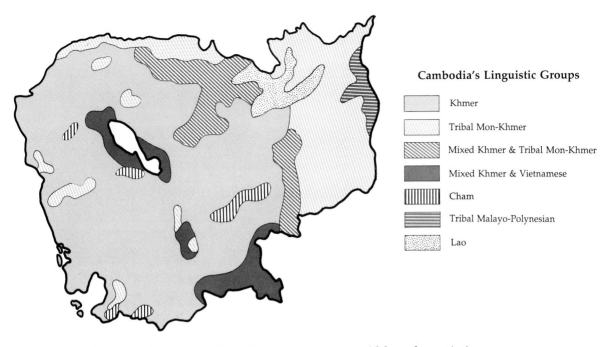

Cambodia's Linguistic Groups

Khmer

Tribal Mon-Khmer

Mixed Khmer & Tribal Mon-Khmer

Mixed Khmer & Vietnamese

Cham

Tribal Malayo-Polynesian

Lao

The population is relatively homogeneous. Although statistics are unreliable, about 80 percent of Cambodia's people would probably classify themselves as Khmer. Minority groups include recent immigrants from Vietnam, thought to number about 300,000, although some estimates run higher; descendants of Chinese immigrants, amounting to perhaps the same number; and smaller numbers of Chams—a Moslem group—and hill tribes, sometimes referred to as *Khmer Loeu* (upper Khmer). Europeans and other foreigners who work in Cambodia are numbered in the hundreds and are almost entirely confined to Phnom Penh or to nearby towns.

Minority Populations

Before the 1970's, Cambodia's minorities lived peacefully alongside the Khmer. Hill people inhabiting the sparsely populated northeastern part of Cambodia were seminomadic hunters and farmers, isolated from other people, while the Cham traditionally specialized in growing cotton and tobacco, silk weaving, raising cattle, and commercial fishing. Traditionally, Chinese and Vietnamese living in Cambodia gravitated toward the towns, where they had been active in commerce, petty trade, and industry. Most of the Chinese came to Cambodia from southeastern China in the nineteenth and twentieth centuries, but we know from earlier accounts that Chinese had settled in Cambodia as merchants as early as seven hundred years ago. Vietnamese immigration is more recent, dating largely from the period when Cambodia, like Vietnam, was a colony of France. During that time, the French encouraged the Vietnamese to settle in Cambodia, believing that they were harder workers than the Khmer and could help the economy to develop. Vietnamese were driven from the country forcibly in 1970 and again in 1975. Since 1979, they have begun drifting back into Cambodia.

Khmer men traditionally preferred careers as farmers, Buddhist monks, or in government service. Khmer women engaged in petty trade, handicrafts, and such home industries as pottery and weaving. In rural areas, of course, men and women worked side by side throughout the agricultural year. Cambodia's rural economy depended on Cambodians for labor and on Chinese and Vietnamese residents to process the crops and sell them in the towns and as exports.

Postrevolutionary Cambodia

The harmony among different groups in Cambodia, evident to visitors in the 1960's, was broken in the 1970's, when nearly all the Vietnamese residents were made to emigrate to Vietnam, a country that most of them had never seen or had fled because of wartime conditions. Under Pol Pot, the remaining Vietnamese were sent off to Vietnam, while Chams were persecuted for their religious beliefs and Chinese were punished for having dominated the economy. As a result of this treatment, tens of thousands of these minorities died during the revolution, and thousands more chose to leave Cambodia soon after the Vietnamese invasion of 1979.

These changes, and the disorder of a decade of war and revolution, altered the ethnic balance in Cambodia and the position of Cambodians in their own society. After the fighting died down and so many men had been killed, thousands of Khmer women, particularly widows, found themselves in jobs traditionally occupied by men—for example, in factories, as village officials, as shopkeepers, and in government departments. Similarly, Cambodian men have found new employment in the cities and along the Thai–Cambodian border as traders, artisans, and shopkeepers, taking jobs formerly held by Chinese and Vietnamese.

In other words, traditional occupational boundaries between different groups, and between men and women, have tended to blur or to dissolve. This trend began soon after the Vietnamese invasion in 1979, when thousands of rural Cambodians streamed into the nearly empty cities and began to rebuild urban life. At the same time many members of minority populations, and what remained of the Cambodian elite, chose to leave Cambodia, where they saw no future for themselves, and moved abroad. Switching places with them were Cambodians with relatively little education, from rural backgrounds, who became city dwellers overnight and were soon coping as best they could with urban living.

In physical terms, Cambodians tend to be huskier, taller, and darker than their counterparts in Thailand, Vietnam, or Laos. Their black hair is often curly, and their eyes are sometimes rounder than those of many people in the region. Looking at sculpture from Cambodia's magnificent Hindu and Buddhist temples, built between A.D. 900 and 1200, it is easy to find men and women who look very much like Cambodians today. Still, it would be hard to say what a "pure" Cambodian looks like. For hundreds of years, and probably for thousands, people with different appearances, customs, and languages have moved across Cambodia or settled in it, including people who might now be citizens of Thailand, Laos, Vietnam, Myanmar, India, and Indonesia. In the nineteenth and twentieth centuries, a good deal of intermarriage took place between Chinese immigrants and the Khmer. Marriages between Khmer and Vietnamese, and between Khmer and Chams, were rare. The descendants of these marriages and of others in the distant past make up the Cambodian "race" today.

Two things bind the Khmer together—their historical experiences and their language.

The Cambodian Language

The *peà-sa khmer* (Khmer language), along with many related dialects and languages, has been spoken in one form or another in Southeast

A farmer in Kompong Speu takes his plow home after a day's work. Sugar palms in the background; in the foreground, a wooden-toothed rake and another farmer's plow.
Christine Drummond

Asia for several thousand years. It belongs to a family of languages called Mon-Khmer. It is a cousin of the languages spoken by some of the hill people of Thailand, Laos, Vietnam, and Malaysia, and of the Mon language, spoken by approximately a million Buddhist rice farmers living in Thailand and southern Myanmar. Linguists have isolated over a hundred distinct Mon-Khmer languages and dialects still being spoken in Southeast Asia, some by only a few hundred people. The isolation of some of these Mon-Khmer–speaking tribes is an indication that Mon-Khmer languages have been spoken in Southeast Asia for longer than many so-called "national" languages, such as Thai and Vietnamese.

Of these related languages, only the Mon and the Khmer themselves have writing systems of their own. These are derived from medieval Indian alphabets, imported into the region along with Indian religious and political ideas by local elites several hundred years ago. Khmer, like English, reads from left to right. Like Thai and Burmese, the Khmer writing system is beautiful to look at, phonetic, and relatively easy to learn, as opposed to Chinese, which has individual characters that must be memorized for every word.

As Cambodia's national language, Khmer is taught in the country's schools and universities and is used in government documents. Although Chinese, Vietnamese, and Chams still speak their own languages, they no longer attend their own schools, as they did in the 1960's, and are gradually being assimilated into the national culture. After years of warfare and neglect, textbooks in Khmer are still rare, and writing and distributing them has been a major task of the government in Phnom Penh. Among educated Cambodians over forty years of age, French is still a second language. In the mid-1980's, however, French was overtaken informally by English as the European language that urban Cambodians wanted to learn. Other foreign languages taught

Khmer

Like all languages spoken today, Khmer has changed over the years, adopting and borrowing words and phrases from other languages, just as English has taken so much of its vocabulary from Latin and Greek; and Khmer continues to borrow words from other languages when they prove useful. In the case of Khmer, most of the borrowing occurred many centuries ago from Sanskrit and Pali, the classical languages of India. These languages have provided Khmer with many abstract words, as well as terms used in politics, literature, and government. Thai, French, and Malay have also given Khmer some of its vocabulary—such as the words for "thirty," "forty," "fifty," and so on (from Chinese, via Thai), the words for "police," "beer," and "field marshal" (from French) and the words for "port" and "market" (from Malay). Not surprisingly, since Chinese have been active in Cambodian commerce for so long, many traditional weights and measures have been borrowed from China. Portuguese traders in the seventeenth century left behind the word for "paper" and the denomination for Cambodian money (the riel, valued in 1989 at about 200 to the U.S. dollar).

Spoken Khmer is vivid and precise. One word, for example, describes the way a small animal, like a rabbit, tucks in one pair of legs when it goes round a corner. The words translated as "mistreat" *(chih cho'an)* actually mean "ride on and kick," and to the verb "to like" *(chole chet)* is literally "to enter the heart." The language also has particular names for over a hundred varieties of rice.

Grammatically, Khmer is relatively simple. There are no tenses, no prefixes or endings, and no "masculine" or "feminine" words. To change the sentence "I go to the market" into past or future, Khmer only adds a word or two indicating the time, like "not yet," "already," or "tomorrow."

The poetic richness of the language comes from its enormous vocabulary, from its often musical sounds, and from its tendency to pile verbs and nouns against each other to achieve a desired poetical effect. Instead of saying "The athlete runs," for example, a Cambodian poet might write something like "The skilled rapid well-built young man speeds galloping past."

Another feature of Cambodian is that it has several different words for "you," depending on the status of the person being addressed. Ordinarily, this status is expressed in family terms (i.e. *bong*, older brother or sister; *om*, elderly uncle; and so on) but there are also special words used for addressing Buddhist monks, children, and members of the royal family. These words were used to locate people either "above" or "below" the person being addressed and displayed respect and condescension, accordingly. Many of these pronouns were forbidden by the Pol Pot government, which sought to place all Cambodians on the same level.

in Cambodian schools in the early 1990's included Russian, Spanish, and Vietnamese. Informal schools for teaching English multiplied in Phnom Penh in anticipation of a tourist boom. In rural areas, where contacts with foreigners are infrequent, nearly everyone speaks only Khmer.

Cambodia's People Today: Boom or Bust?

Since the early 1980's, foreign journalists and most other visitors have not been allowed to circulate freely in Cambodia, because of the threats posed by guerrillas and because the Phnom Penh government, like many others in the past, has preferred to control the information about Cambodia that reaches the outside world. This makes it difficult to say much about social and economic conditions in many rural areas today, as compared with those in Phnom Penh or in the places where visitors are usually taken. Even in the cities, some see hopeful new prosperity and others a frightening descent into corruption and despair.

At the same time, some statements about Cambodia today are easy to make. The first, already emphasized, is that nearly all its people are desperately poor. By the early 1990's, agricultural production has not yet reached prerevolutionary levels, and indeed it seems likely that in many war-torn and forested areas little food is being grown. Malnutrition is a serious problem in many parts of the country and is the major illness treated in the children's hospital in Phnom Penh. Other diseases, such as malaria and tuberculosis, are widespread in rural areas. Many parts of the country are too embattled for people to be sure of eating the food they grow, and refugees from these areas, particularly widows and single mothers with small children, eke out precarious livings in Phnom Penh, often finding it difficult to cope.

A bicyclist pulls heavy rolls of straw matting through a rainstorm in Phnom Penh. Rainfall in Cambodia is heavy, but storms are relatively brief. Christine Drummond

Yet some parts of the country, such as Kompong Chhnang on the shores of the Tonle Sap, have regained some of their earlier prosperity, as fisheries have reopened and a flourishing trade in fish and fish products has developed between Cambodia and southern Vietnam. Similarly, in the ruby and sapphire mining regions of the northwest, many individual miners have become wealthy by trading across the border with Thailand. Similar fortunes are being made by Khmer and Thai who cooperate, without official permission, to cut down valuable timber in the frontier region. Still other Cambodians, transporting goods from Thailand through Cambodia to Vietnam by truck, on foot, or on bicycles, earn a handsome profit, and there is a flourishing coastal trade in Cambodia's "Wild West" province of Koh Kong.

Main boulevards in Phnom Penh, 1988, early morning. The Central Market, built in the 1930's, is visible at the rear.   Christine Drummond

Hardly any of this prosperity reaches the Phnom Penh government in the form of taxes, and the government is therefore sorely pressed to provide basic services like electricity, water, and sanitation to its people—to say nothing of education, new roads, or proper medical care. The new prosperity does "trickle down" to many poor Cambodians who find jobs in building construction, restaurants, tourist services, and markets unthinkable in the more austerely socialist atmosphere of the early 1980's. As Vietnamese troops departed, and the government relaxed its dependence on Vietnam, it became unclear to what extent any Cambodian government could influence events outside the capital, or control the economic boom that seemed to have overtaken Phnom Penh.

Benefits are very uneven, and many Cambodians in the 1980's balanced on a thin edge between death and survival. Hundreds of thousands of them had too little to eat, worked long hours for pitiful rewards, and succumbed easily to disease. These hardships darkened the picture of an economic boom based on trade and speculation, reported by many visitors to Phnom Penh and to areas along the Thai border.

This "boom," if it really is one, is based largely on informal trade with Thailand and between Thailand and Vietnam, and also on increasing revenue from tourism, real estate speculation, and the possibility of renewed foreign investment, particularly by Thailand, Hong Kong, and Japan. With the relaxation of Vietnamese influence, many Cambodian government officials have become wealthy, as have individual traders, themselves often Vietnamese, Chinese, or Chinese-Cambodians.

Prospects for the Future

These developments have also widened the gaps between Cambodia's rich and poor, and, some would say, between the Vietnamese and Chinese minorities on the one hand and Cambodia's urban and rural poor on the other. Some visitors saw the changes as evidence of a new openness and new opportunities for Cambodia, and as a chance for Khmers to benefit from relative political freedom and from the prosperity of the early 1990's. The rebirth of Buddhism, and Buddhist festivals, was seen by many as a hopeful sign and as evidence of the resilience of Cambodian culture and the flexibility of its supposedly Communist leaders. Others claimed that the collapse of the old monarchy, the pressures of world economics, and Cambodia's hardships in the 1970's and early 1980's had all been too much for the country, and that its very survival was in doubt.

Still others perceived the changes in the late 1980's as a return to the widespread corruption of prerevolutionary times, when gaps developed between the richest and poorest members of Cambodian society, and particularly between high officials in the government and ordinary people. Some resented the favored treatment they claimed was being given to the Vietnamese inhabitants of the country. In the 1970's, similar injustice led many young people to join the revolutionary forces led by Pol Pot. After the "killing fields" of the early 1970's, sweeping social change was no longer a real possibility, but if widespread corruption continues, it could easily erode the confidence that has been built up in the 1980's between the government and the people.

These economic threats, changes, and opportunities, as well as the evolving relationship between the government and the people, must be seen, in the short term, against the background of an ongoing civil war and in the context of the economic boom that has overtaken so much of the region. The future will also be affected by the breakdown of Communist parties in Europe and the pressure against those that survive in Asia, especially in China and Vietnam. If Cambodia is to become a non-Communist country, as seems likely, what kind of government will it have?

In the longer term, the rapid changes of the 1980's need to be seen in the context of Cambodia's history, for which written records extend back for nearly two thousand years.

Cambodia's Early History

Prehistoric Cambodia

Since World War II, great advances have been made in the study of prehistoric Southeast Asia. Not much of this work has been carried out in Cambodia itself, but what is known about prehistoric civilizations in present-day Thailand and Vietnam helps define what life was like in Cambodia before the appearance of written records, roughly two thousand years ago.

The earliest site excavated in Cambodia so far is Laang Spean cave, in the northwest. Archaeologists estimate that the cave was occupied, or at least visited, by human beings on and off between around 7000 B.C. and approximately A.D. 700. Animal bones found in the cave indicate that these early people survived by hunting and gathering their food rather than by growing crops. Hunters and gatherers, who still survive in parts of Southeast Asia, Australia, Africa, and South America, travel from place to place seeking food in different seasons. There were hunter-gatherers in Cambodia as recently as the 1960's, particularly in the hills of the northeast. In the 1970's, many city dwellers, exiled to Cambodia's inhospitable forests, were forced to learn the skills of their ancestors in gathering edible plants, wild honey, small reptiles, and other animals.

At some point around 2000 B.C., Southeast Asians began to cultivate rice and to gather into permanent village settlements. Pottery, which is rare among hunter-gatherers even today, came into use at about the same time. The settlements were usually located near the sea or some other body of water, which could be drawn on for irrigation, drinking, and washing. Burial sites excavated in such sites indicate that some inhabitants or families enjoyed higher status than others. In one such site in Thailand, a woman was buried about 3000 years ago with over 100,000 ornamental beads.

Soon after the introduction of agriculture and pottery came the appearance of metal—bronze at first, followed by iron. Those skilled in making metal often enjoyed high status, and metal objects such as axes, drums, and gongs were often used in religious ceremonies rather than for everyday work. Because deposits of tin, lead and copper ore, needed to make bronze, were often far apart, and far from the places where bronze objects have been found, the appearance of metal, around 1500 B.C., must have come at a time when extensive trading networks already existed in mainland Southeast Asia.

Samrong Sen

A bronze-age settlement at Samrong Sen, near Kŏmpong Chhnang, was excavated by French archaeologists in the 1870's. Their findings indi-

Time Line

c. 5000 B.C.: Evidence of cave-dwelling people in northwestern Cambodia.

c. 1000 B.C.: Bronze-casting culture centered on Samrong Sen.

c. 200 B.C.–A.D. 200: Trading center of Oc-Eo, on South Vietnamese coast, flourishes, while inland kingdoms known by Chinese as "Funan" send tribute to China. This period also marked by early stages of Indianization of Cambodia. Beginnings of writing; implantation of Hindu religion.

Fifth century A.D.: First stone inscriptions in Sanskrit and Khmer in Cambodia. Kingdoms known by Chinese as "Zhen-la" send tribute to the Chinese court.

802: King Jayavarman II inaugurates dynasty in northwestern Cambodia.

802–1431: Hindu-Buddhist kingdom known today as Angkor flourishes in northwestern Cambodia. Its influence extends into present-day Thailand, Laos, and Vietnam.

c. 1130: King Suryavarman II builds Angkor Wat, still the largest religious building in the world.

1178–1220: Jayavarman VII, a Buddhist monarch, reigns at Angkor, builds Bayon and other temples. At his death, stone constructions cease, and inscriptions become rare.

1296: Chinese diplomat, Chou Ta-kuan, visits Angkor and reports his observations.

cate that around 2000 B.C., the people living at Samrong Sen knew how to cast bronze and had already domesticated cattle, pigs, and water buffaloes. Their diet, like that of Cambodians today, consisted primarily of rice and fish. Their houses, also like Cambodian houses today, were raised on posts. Human skeletons showed that they were the same physical types as contemporary Cambodians. The settlement resembled others excavated in recent years in central and northeastern Thailand, and pottery found there resembled pottery excavated in those places and in Vietnam.

Between 600 and 400 B.C., archaeologists now believe, ironworking became widespread on the Southeast Asian mainland. The introduction of iron-tipped plows, which overturn more soil, greatly increased rice production. Soon afterward, Indian and Chinese traders and colonists came into contact with the region. Evidence comes from Indian and Chinese goods buried in Southeast Asian tombs, and from the introduction of Chinese agricultural and metal-casting technologies in northern Vietnam.

It is likely that settlements in Cambodia in this period resembled those excavated in northeastern Thailand. These were often circular or oval in shape, surrounded by moats and embankments. One large settlement recently excavated in northeast Thailand housed about a thousand people about two thousand years ago, before the appearance of any "kingdoms" in the region.

The First Cambodian Kingdoms

By A.D. 400, the first Southeast Asian kingdoms appeared. Increased rice production freed some people to engage in other work, such as elaborate boat building, house decoration, bronze manufacture, and making arrangements for feasting. Others were freed to be soldiers, and a few became priests and rulers. These men soon became the most honored people in society. Often they demonstrated their power by the size of their followings and the amount of their wealth. In Cambodia, they claimed that they were descended from the *neak ta* (ancestral figures) who had been the first settlers in a given region. The ancestors, in turn, were seen as responsible for a community's well-being, expressed in terms of agricultural production, peace, and good health. Those who claimed high status demonstrated it by sponsoring feasts and by displaying their accumulated wealth which in the case of chieftains often included several wives, married to form alliances between families from different villages. There is no evidence, however, that these societies were literate or that they drew their inspiration from abroad.

It was at this stage that Indian traders and missionaries, in small numbers at first, began to appear on the Southeast Asian mainland in search of spices, tropical birds, ivory, rhinoceros horns, and other forest products. Another important export from Southeast Asia at this time was gold and precious stones; from the earliest times, the region was known in India as Suvarnabhumi (The Golden Land). Naturally, the first contacts occurred in coastal areas. Unfortunately, written records of these early visits have not survived.

Funan

The coastline of what is now southern Vietnam, then inhabited by Khmer, made an ideal stopping place, where traders "turned the corner" of Southeast Asia as they plied between the Roman Empire, India, and China, hugging the coasts where possible. Because of the monsoons, Indian ships that reached Southeast Asia often had to stay for several months, waiting for the prevailing winds to change. It is likely that during these layovers, local chieftains became interested in certain

Indian practices, such as those that measured the solar year and others that set priests and chieftains above and apart from the rest of society, by means of a system of ranks, or castes. Chiefs were also interested in technology useful for the royal displays of grandeur that were made possible by gold working and silk weaving. Buddhist monks also passed through Southeast Asia at this time, en route from centers of Buddhist learning in India to China, and local rulers often were impressed by Buddhist teachings.

Cambodia has a legend that traces its origin to the marriage of a foreigner from India and a locally born dragon princess. One version suggests that an Indian priest named Kaundinya, armed with a magical bow, appeared one day off the shore of Cambodia. The dragon princess, in a dugout, paddled to meet him. The priest shot an arrow into her boat and frightened her into marrying him. Her father, the dragon king, "enlarged the possessions of his son-in-law," the legend says, "by drinking up the water that covered the country. He later built them a capital, and changed the name of the country to Cambodia." The dragon king's action may be a reference to the drainage canals that were built in the Mekong Delta of southern Vietnam perhaps in the second century A.D. and are still visible from the air. "Cambodia" (sometimes spelled Kambuja or Kampuchea) was the name of an area of northern India.

Chinese visitors in the third century A.D. first reported this legend but called the coastal kingdom "Funan." Another version of the legend says that Kaundinya was the founder of the country and goes on to say: "The people of Funan heard of him. The whole kingdom rose with joy. They came to him and chose him king. He changed its rules to follow the customs of India."

Roman coins from the second century A.D. have been found in excavations at Oc-Eo in southern Vietnam, at approximately the location where the seacoast is estimated to have been eighteen centuries ago, but there is nothing from Oc-Eo to link it with Funan. Other finds have included

Indian jewelry, gems, glass beads, bronzeware, and local pottery. Funan sent tributary gifts to China between A.D. 250 and 519, but there is no archaeological evidence of such a powerful, centralized kingdom anywhere in the region at this time. Probably Funan was a loose federation of coastal settlements, with several local chieftains, allied with inland groups of villages, who may have called themselves "kings" while writing to the Chinese court. A Chinese visitor in the fourth century A.D. reported that:

The houses are covered with leaves of a plant which grows on the edge of the sea. . . . The leaves are six to seven feet long, and take the form of a fish. The king rides mounted on an elephant. The [royal] women also ride elephants. His subjects are ugly and black. Their hair is frizzy. They wear neither clothing nor shoes. For a living, they cultivate the soil.

The visitor added that "the barbarians are not without their own history books; they even have libraries for them."

Indianization

By the third century A.D., Indian influence in the form of writing was already widespread in Funan, whose inhabitants were farmers, making their houses from palm leaves as they do today. Unfortunately, there is almost no other firsthand information about this period, when Cambodians encountered Indians and responded to them by absorbing some of their ideas, blending others with their own, and sharing technological skills.

The process of Indianization continued for several centuries in Cambodia. Those most affected by it were members of the elite, who gave themselves Indian names, composed poetry in Indian languages, and followed the spiritual guidance of Indian *Brahmins* (priests). Indian religion, stressing the worship of such gods as Shiva and Vishnu, blended with local beliefs, particularly in ancestors and in spirits of the

Hinduism and Buddhism

These two religions reached Cambodia about two thousand years ago. Both originated in India, and both played important parts in the social and ideological life of early Cambodian kingdoms.

Buddhism, like Christianity and Islam, is based on the teachings of a historical figure, Gautama, known as the Buddha, or Enlightened One. Gautama, born a prince in northern India in the sixth century B.C., spent much of his life contemplating the meaning of existence, which he connected with suffering. He taught that by proper behavior and thinking, individuals could overcome suffering and obtain enlightenment. The Buddha made no claims that he was divine. His teaching, transmitted largely by Buddhist monks, was in essence a set of methods by which individuals could become enlightened.

Buddhism flourished in Cambodia in the sixth and seventh centuries A.D., and again after about 1200, when a king at Angkor, Jayavarman VII, embraced its teachings. Jayavarman followed the so-called Great Vehicle brand of Buddhism (Mahayana), still practiced in China, Japan, Vietnam, and Tibet. By about 1300, influenced by missionaries from Burma and Siam, most Cambodians practiced Hinayana, or Lesser Vehicle Buddhism, which was more austere than Mahayana. This branch of Buddhism has flourished ever since in Cambodia, Laos, Thailand, Myanmar, and Sri Lanka.

In modern Cambodia, Buddhist life centered around religious festivals held at the *wat* (monastery) throughout the year. Buddhist monks are held in high esteem, and many Cambodian men try to enter monastic life for a short period before they get married.

In the Communist revolution in 1975–1978, *wat*s were destroyed and monks were forced to become farm laborers. Buddhism revived in the 1980's in Cambodia, but in recent times it has not been as popular among ordinary Cambodians as it was before the revolution.

Hinduism, unlike Buddhism, is a religion filled with good and evil gods. These include Shiva, the god of creativity and destruction; Vishnu, the patron of kings; their wives, Durga and Uma; the elephant god, Ganesa; and Kali, the goddess of death, to name a few. The priests of Hindusim are the so-called *Brahmins,* supposedly those at the top level of society, which is divided into several levels, or castes. The caste system, which persists in India today, did not catch hold in medieval Cambodia, but many Hindu gods were popular there, and the carvings at Angkor often depict them, as well as scenes from Indian mythology. Most Angkorean inscriptions are in Sanskrit, the Indian language associated with Brahmanism.

Cambodian classical literature and the royal classical dance draw on Hindu models, such as the *Ramayana*, the ancient epic that recounts the travels of an Indian prince searching for his wife and doing battle with evil kings.

Hinduism and Buddhism flourished side by side in medieval Cambodia. The two religions, with their emphasis on other-worldliness, were spurned by Cambodia's revolutionaries, but Buddhist teaching and Indian mythology continue to play important parts in Cambodian culture.

A Cambodian inscription (eighth century A.D.). Cambodian script, originally from India, was modified over the centuries, but many of the letters in this inscription are legible to Cambodians today.   Claude Jacques

soil, believed to be responsible for the kingdom's welfare and prosperity. Before long, local rulers were identifying themselves with Indian gods, and the gods themselves were seen as in some way linked with local ancestor spirits. Indian texts dealing with government organization and kingship were understandably popular with these petty rulers.

The archaeological record of this period is thin, as few inscriptions were carved in stone, and almost no stone buildings or sculptures have survived. It seems likely that nearly all the buildings and statues in this period were made of wood or other perishable materials, as they are in the Cambodian countryside today.

Zhen-la

It is difficult to trace the transition from what the Chinese called "Funan" to a second kingdom farther inland, to which they referred, beginning in the seventh century A.D., as "Zhen-la." There was probably no kingdom of that name. Archaeological evidence points to the existence of several small city-states in the Mekong River basin between the fifth and eighth centuries A.D. These were located for the most part alongside navigable streams. In this period other Indianized kingdoms appeared along the coasts of Southeast Asia and on the island of Java in Indonesia. Indian priests, scholars, and merchants, and Southeast Asians, traveled between these kingdoms and pooled their knowledge.

The earliest Khmer-language inscriptions date from the seventh century A.D. While those in Sanskrit, almost always in verse, praise the activities of priests and rulers, the Khmer-language inscriptions, written in prose, commemorate transactions involving land, slaves, temples, and reservoirs. In the early seventh century, these reservoirs, or ponds,

Eighth-century statues abandoned in the forest in Kompong Cham. Before the 1970's, statues like these, considered semisacred, were seldom disturbed. More recently, many of them have been smuggled out of Cambodia and sold for high prices to collectors and museums in foreign countries. Author

were controlled by people with the title *pon*; by the eighth century, these figures had been replaced by apparently high-ranking ones with Sanskrit names, and sometimes bearing royal titles.

These men had control over specific regions, or more precisely over the people in those regions, because controlling labor to grow rice, rather than land by itself, was the key to a ruler's power. The leaders frequently fought each other, hoping to take prisoners and loot, thereby proving to their own subjects that they were rulers worthy of their ancestors and capable of providing protection. Unfortunately, all wars had losers, and many of the small kingdoms known collectively as Zhen-la disappeared when their people were evacuated to serve the kings who had won.

The process of centralization meant more extensive public works, larger stone buildings, and more elaborate inscriptions—all indications that a ruler had rice surpluses, and many workers, at his disposal.

The temples were usually dedicated to the Hindu deity Shiva and, more rarely, to Vishnu. They were relatively small, housing statues of the gods, embodying the potency of male ancestors on the one hand and insuring the fertility of the soil, perceived as female, on the other. Local kings also identified themselves with Shiva. Unlike Buddhist temples later on, these Hindu temples were accessible only to priests. On the surrounding land, subsistence farmers were required to work several days a month to serve the temples—growing food, making repairs, or preparing for the elaborate festivals conducted at various points in the agricultural year.

Archaeological work on sites associated with Zhen-la has been delayed by war and political instability and has lagged behind work carried out in sites from the same period in China, Thailand, and Vietnam. Nineteenth- and twentieth-century French archaeologists, fascinated by the artistic grandeur of medieval Cambodia, went looking for important kings and concentrated on studying major religious sites, where buildings were made of stone and where royal activities, or those of priests, were commemorated by stone inscriptions. The influence of India was exaggerated, and local initiative was played down. As a result, hardly any work has been done to excavate medieval villages, quarries, cemeteries, or trading centers. Such work, when carried out, will be helpful in demonstrating the links that existed between kingdoms in what is now Cambodia and similar kingdoms, some populated by Khmer, in Thailand, Laos, and Vietnam.

Most inscriptions commemorate the actions of the elite; those in Sanskrit, praising kings, portray them as supernatural figures. This yields a top-heavy view of early Cambodian society, which fails to note the contributions of low-born men and women. Their main obvious contribution was that they were the ancestors of today's Khmer, and helped to transmit Cambodian culture, the Khmer language, and Cambodian responses to the landscape from one generation to the next.

The tendency to concentrate on Cambodian royalty, and the grandeur of the state, becomes more pronounced in the so-called "Angkorean" era, which stretches between Jayavarman's victories in the early ninth century and the middle of the fifteenth. During these years, a mighty kingdom came into being in northwestern Cambodia, expanded, stabilized, lost wars, and eventually collapsed.

Its center lay near the present-day village of Siem Reap, just beyond the flood limits of the Tonle Sap. Its magnificent temples, sculptures, bridges, inscriptions, and irrigation works—in other words, everything that survives that was made of stone—testify to its having been one of the major cities of the world and certainly the most powerful state, for a time, on the mainland of Southeast Asia. It can be argued that Cambodia reached its peak in the twelfth century, when its most impressive temple, Angkor Wat, was erected. Very few countries can claim such a rich archaeological heritage.

Kingship and Society at Angkor

The Early Stages

The Cambodian word *angkor* derives from the Sanskrit word *nagara*, meaning "holy city," and is used as the name for the civilization that flourished in northwestern Cambodia and northeastern Thailand between the beginning of the ninth century A.D. and the middle of the fifteenth century. The remains of this civilization include several hundred archaeological sites in Cambodia itself, and over a thousand Khmer and Sanskrit inscriptions (including pre-Angkorean ones) from Cambodia, Thailand, and Laos. From these, scholars have identified twenty-six distinct Angkorean kings, who ruled between 802 and approximately 1300, when stone inscriptions cease.

The founder of Angkor was a king named Jayavarman (reigned 802–834) who left no inscriptions of his own. But a good deal is known about him from inscriptions carved by others. He seems to have been a Cambodian regional chief, with some supposedly royal ancestry, who spent much of his early life as a student or a prisoner somewhere in present-day Indonesia. When he returned to Cambodia around 770, he fought a series of campaigns to consolidate his control over different parts of the country. These took Jayavarman through southwestern, central, and northwestern Cambodia, gradually subduing local chiefs, on whom he bestowed royal titles and who offered female relatives to him as wives. In 802, on Kulen mountain to the north of present-day Angkor, he participated in a ceremony that identified him with the Hindu god Shiva and entitled him to the name of *chakravartin* (universal monarch). The ceremony, which opened the "Angkorean" era, was reenacted by Cambodian kings for at least 250 years.

Soon afterward, Jayavarman moved his capital down onto the plain, to the site known as Roluos, east of Angkor, where it was to remain for most of the rest of the ninth century.

The next two kings consolidated the process of centralization, and kept their capital at Roluos, where several brick temples, a large reservoir, and a "temple-mountain"—the first to be made of stone rather than brick—have survived. In 889, King Yasovarman I transferred the capital to the site of present-day Angkor, centering his city around another temple-mountain, built on top of a hill, and known today as Phnom Bakheng (Mount Mighty Ancestor). This temple was much larger and more complicated than its predecessor at Roluos. To the east of the mountain, Yasovarman built a reservoir roughly four miles long and two miles wide (about six by three kilometers)—an effort that must have called on a far larger labor pool than any previous public work. He also ordered the construction of temple-mountains elsewhere in Cambodia and in what is now northeastern Thailand, then probably still inhabited by Khmer. In one of his inscriptions, in fact, he claimed that his kingdom was bordered by "the Chinese frontier and the sea."

Yasovarman's inscriptions reveal his courtiers' talent for flattery, as well as the grand ideas that Cambodian kings had about themselves. Two stanzas from the long inscription at Lolei, a temple dedicated to his parents, boast that:

He spread his favors on the world, without asking anything in exchange; has anyone seen the sun asking the lotus to open its flowers?
In all the sciences and martial arts, in art, languages, and writing, in dancing, singing, and everything else, [Yasovarman] was as skilled as if he had created them.

Building at Angkor

Cambodian kings who enjoyed long, prosperous reigns, like Yasovarman I, followed a set pattern of building activity. First they dammed up local streams to form large rectangular reservoirs, or lakes. This provided water for irrigating the surrounding ricefields, and canals leading out of it provided waterways for moving goods and people.

The next step was to build a temple-pyramid in the middle of the lake, representing Mount Meru, the home of the Hindu gods, and housing images of the king's parents and other ancestors, often disguised as Hindu gods. Later on, perhaps when they sensed their reigns drawing to a close, the kings built temple-tombs for themselves, also modeled after Mount Meru, and surrounded by moats. Some kings died or were overthrown before they could complete their projects. In other reigns, shifts of population, wars, or epidemics may have slowed down the kings, or prevented them from carrying out their plans. But at least

Guardian maiden, Mount Bakheng (ninth century A.D.). This temple-mountain, built by King Yasovarman I, was the first major temple in the Angkor region. H. Roger-Viollet

thirteen of the twenty-six Angkorean kings are known to have built temple-mountains.

To ordinary Cambodians, these enormous buildings and reservoirs demonstrated the grandeur, remoteness, and divinity of kings. In Angkorean times, many of the statues were painted or gilded, and the towers and doorways were sheathed with copper or bronze. Looking up at the temples or seeing them reflected in the reservoirs and moats, and watching religious festivals conducted by Brahmin priests, who chanted prayers in Indian languages, must have given these men and women a sense of a magical, slightly menacing world far beyond their own capacities and expectations.

Kingship and the People

Like the priests, the kings, their wives, and their attendants didn't grow their own food. Hidden behind gilded walls, they wore silks and gold jewelry, and when they emerged were carried from place to place by slaves, or rode on elephants. Instead of eating, they feasted. Their orders had to be obeyed; hundreds if not thousands of ordinary people were at their beck and call. Their actions were thought of as "royal," or "priestly," rather than merely human, and a separate vocabulary developed in Cambodian to describe them.

Other aspects of priestly and royal conduct set them apart from everyday life. Their temples were the only buildings in Cambodia made of stone. Everything else was made of perishable material—wood, thatch, and bamboo. The carvings on the temples represented the world of the Indian gods, Indian myths, and ancient Indian epic poems, particularly the *Mahabharata* and the *Ramayana*, familiar to Cambodians from as early as the sixth century A.D.. The temple-mountains, finally, were made to resemble Mount Meru, the mythical home of the gods, supposedly in the snow-covered Himalayan mountains of northern

The temple of Lolei (Roluos, ninth century A.D.), right, alongside a modern-day Cambodian Buddhist monastery, or wat. H. Roger-Viollet

Demons, Bakong (Roluos, ninth century A.D.). Bulging eyes, long hair, and exposed, sharp teeth mark these faces as demonic. The small figure in the foreground may be a human being condemned to the the demons' realm.   Walter Veit

India, thousands of miles from the Tonle Sap. To many Cambodians, looking up from sunbaked or waterlogged fields and from their back-breaking work of plowing, transplanting, and harvesting, these fantastic buildings, the Hindu gods, and the elegant people who benefited from them were symbols of another world.

The farmers' own supernatural world, in the form of ancestral spirits, was never far away. Cambodia was crowded with such spirits—the founders of villages, dead heroes, those associated with particular places, and the ancestors of kings, to name a few. Some of these were thought to be kind; others were evil. Like gods everywhere, they accepted praise, sacrifices, and gifts. In the nineteenth century, these were offered by families, in villages, and at many levels of society, finally by Brahmin priests in royal temples.

These practices were inherited from Angkorean times. Certainly in that era it was the Brahmins' job to deal with the Indian-named deities who protected the king, and the kingdom of Kambuja. These gods, and Shiva in particular, played the same roles for the nation as ancestral spirits played in individual villages.

The king's job was to mediate among these competing gods and to assure the fertility of the soil, the prosperity of his people, and the arrival of rain at the proper time. This association between the king and the weather lasted for hundreds of years. In the 1940's and 1950's, the Cambodian king, Norodom Sihanouk, was thought by many rural people to have the power to influence the seasons.

Kings and priests were distant, foreign, and "above" ordinary people; at the same time, by their supernatural powers, they were closely linked with people's everyday life. The kingdom survived with the permission of those ancestors who lived on beneath the earth. This permission was obtained through ceremonies connected with, or carried out by, the king. Without a king, and without such expressions of his grandeur as temple-mountains to house his body when he died and became an ancestor-spirit, it was thought that the country would collapse.

This does not mean that Cambodia in Angkorean times, or indeed at any time in its history, was always or even often at peace. Its political arrangements seem to have been fragile, and great efforts were always needed to keep outlying areas, to say nothing of the king's own relatives, under control. Over and over in Cambodia's long history, usurpers seized power, or failed to do so, after ruinous civil wars.

Royal Politics

Royal politics were unstable. One reason for this was that kings often had many wives and dozens of children. Some wives were preferred over others. They hoped to place their sons in powerful positions and to see that their daughters married powerful men. Their brothers and uncles, meanwhile, often carved out portions of the kingdom to run more or less as their own. In the tenth century, an Angkorean king tried to reduce the power of these local "kings" by changing their realms into provinces and drawing the leaders into the capital, where they could be more closely supervised. In the early eleventh century, if not before, these officials were made to swear an oath of allegiance to the king. In exchange, they were formally granted territories to govern.

When a king died, provincial rulers usually owed no loyalty to his successor. Moreover, the throne didn't pass automatically to the monarch's eldest son. Only eight of the twenty-six Angkorean kings succeeded their fathers or their brothers. The other kings were outsiders, or nephews, grandchildren, and cousins of the preceding king. Nearly all of these men must have fought their way to power, either by manipulating the political system or by resorting to civil war. Surviving inscriptions, which are concerned with a given ruler's glory and success, tell us little about these struggles for power or about everyday political life. Once a king had died, even if he had been killed by his successor, he was honored in ceremonies and was made into a semidivine protector of the kingdom, a royal ancestor-spirit.

Building Angkor

In this context, it is amazing that so much work was accomplished at Angkor. Constructing the reservoirs and monuments often took as long as twenty years, for laborers could be recruited in large numbers only between agricultural seasons, and building was often delayed or interrupted as workers were asked to serve as soldiers or as crises of royal succession occupied the elite. In other words, work could only proceed when the kingdom was prosperous and at peace. At such times, thousands of skilled and unskilled workers were needed for the projects. These had to be brought in from surrounding villages, from villages housing prisoners of war, and from the hills to the north of Angkor. The work of assembling, feeding, and organizing this labor force, as well as arranging for transport, tools, and materials, including tons of stone brought from quarries to the north of the city, must have been daunting. So were the problems of coordinating artists and artisans, and making the precise measurements necessary for monuments often built on an enormous scale.

And while the outward lives of farmers and ordinary people can be reconstructed from carvings on some of the temples, and royal activities from the same carvings and from inscriptions, it is more difficult to resurrect the lives of the Angkorean professional class. These included the largely anonymous architects, officials, and engineers who designed the temples, organized the work forces, commanded the armies, and supervised the construction of the reservoirs, roads, and canals. It seems likely that many of them owed their status and education to royal or priestly connections; certainly only the children of privileged Cambodians had access to education. On the other hand, girls from less privileged backgrounds were often chosen as wives of kings and princes, and their children, whose grandparents might have been illiterate, joined the elite.

Similarly, since only stone inscriptions from Angkor have survived, we know nothing about the poets, historians, and scribes whose work was written on leather (as in the European Middle Ages) or on bamboo. Chinese visitors observed that the Khmer maintained historical records, but all of these from the Angkorean period have been lost. Khmer-

language inscriptions reveal that there were complicated rules governing land ownership, taxes, and the administration of Hindu and Buddhist temples. These suggest that offices, libraries, and archives were needed to keep the day-to-day records of the kingdom. Because these records have disappeared, some very basic questions about Angkor, such as how many people it contained, or how rich it was in present-day monetary terms, can never be answered. Little has been determined about the ethnic composition of the city or about the nature and extent of manufacturing or foreign trade. Instead, historians are left with a top-heavy, royally oriented picture of Cambodian society, and the misleading impression that Angkorean civilization consisted of erecting enormous religious buildings.

Angkor: The Middle Period

After Yasovarman I's death in 910, the kings at Angkor for the next two hundred years, as far as their activities can be reconstructed, followed the patterns laid down by the founders of the civilization, whom they took pains to honor. As time went on, the landscape around Angkor was covered with small and large stone temples. Aerial photographs reveal that the region also was crisscrossed with reservoirs, roads, and canals. The temples honored kings and occasionally high-ranking families. They provided work and shelter for Hindu priests, Buddhist monks, and the people who grew food for them, carved statues, and provided other services. The roads and canals connected the city with rice-growing areas and enabled officials and armies to travel to these regions to collect taxes, recruit laborers, and put down revolts.

Guardian, Preah Ko (Roluos, ninth century A.D.). Carrying a trident, this fierce warrior wears several jeweled belts and pendant earrings. Walter Veit

The canals, as in medieval China, also transported officials, workers, and visitors, as well as agricultural and other goods, to the capital city. Aerial photography has revealed one such canal, now silted over, that ran, straight as an arrow, for forty miles (sixty-four kilometers) between Angkor and another ruined city to the east.

Scholars have reconstructed the activities of several monarchs from this period, while others seem to have sunk without a trace. Some of the kings expanded control over outlying districts, and were renowned for their learning or for their patronage of the arts. They supervised the construction of temples, roads, and irrigation works. These activities are celebrated in their inscriptions. Other kings left few inscriptions or buildings behind them, and in some cases we can infer that their reigns were marked by crises and disorder.

Two of the most important kings at Angkor were Suryavarman I, who reigned from 1002 to 1050, and Suryavarman II, who reigned from 1113 to 1150. The first is important because of his work at centralizing political and religious power at Angkor; the second is famous largely because his temple-mountain, Angkor Wat, is the largest and best known of all the Angkorean buildings.

Suryavarman I (his name means "protected by the sun"), like Jayavarman II, was an outsider, who reached the throne following a series of military campaigns and alliances with powerful local leaders. It was nine years before he took possession of Angkor itself. He claimed descent from a ninth-century Cambodian king, suggesting that his connections with the preceding monarch were remote. He also differed from many Cambodian kings by being a patron of Buddhism rather than Hinduism.

Suryavarman I expanded the Angkorean empire. He was responsible for building temples in southwestern Cambodia and in what is now northeastern Thailand, right on the Cambodian border, and southern

Laos. His inscriptions have been found as far away as Lop Buri, north of Bangkok. At Angkor itself, he greatly expanded the irrigation system. One reservoir, the largest that has survived, covered approximately 10 square miles (26 square kilometers), and held over 150 million gallons (570 million liters) of water. At the end of his long reign, rebellions broke out in several regions. The remainder of the eleventh century seems to have been a period of instability.

Suryavarman II was not a direct descendant of Suryavarman I, but like him he was a usurper, seizing power in 1113, allegedly after killing a rival prince in battle: "Jumping onto the head of the elephant belonging to the enemy king, he killed him as [an eagle] on the slope of a mountain might kill a snake."

Angkor Wat, the largest religious building in the world, was built in the twelfth century A.D. by King Suryavarman II. Its towers have figured in all Cambodian flags since the 1950's, when Cambodia gained its independence from France. Angkor Wat is considered by many to be one of the architectural wonders of the world. Charles F. Keyes

Angkor Wat

His temple-mountain, Angkor Wat, is the largest religious building in the world, and the most famous of the temples in Cambodia. It differs from others at Angkor by facing west instead of east, and by being dedicated to Vishnu rather than to Shiva. It probably served as Surya-varman's tomb and seems to have been completed soon after his death in 1150.

Angkor Wat is surrounded by a moat over 200 yards (182 meters) wide. Like other temple-mountains, its five towers are meant to resemble Mount Meru, the home of the gods, surrounded by an ocean. The moat and outer wall enclose almost a square mile (2.6 square kilometers) of territory.

After crossing the moat, visitors encounter a covered gallery, running on four sides of an inner courtyard. Its walls are covered with over half a mile (.8 kilometer) of carvings, representing scenes from Indian epics, from myths about Vishnu, and from Suryavarman's life, in particular his military campaigns against the emerging state of Vietnam to the east and the Hindu kingdom of Champa. Graceful *apsara* (celestial dancers), carved in half-relief, cover the outer walls. Other stretches of wall are carved with leaf patterns and floral decorations.

Scholars have recently discovered that Angkor Wat served as a place from which astronomers could observe the movements of the sun, moon, and stars. It has also been argued that the key measurements of the temple are based on Cambodian ideas of time, derived from India.

According to Hindu belief, the earth will last for 4.3 billion years, divided into four *yuga* (ages). Nine tenths of this time has already elapsed. We are living in the last and shortest era, known as the *kaliyuga*, at the end of which the world will be destroyed, and when a new world will take its place. The distances between elements of the temple, running from west to east, measured in *hat* (a distance of roughly half a yard), coincide with the length of the remaining 43 million years, divided by 1,000—that is, 43,000 *hat* or about ten miles.

Entering the temple, heading east by crossing the moat, a visitor travels forward in space but symbolically backward in time, from the present era toward the earliest one. Known as the *kritayuga,* this period is thought of as a golden age when gods and men inhabited the world together. The beginning of the walk, thus, occurs in the final, destructive era. At the end, a visitor originally saw the statue of Vishnu, since disappeared, that was in the central sanctuary of the temple and was identified with Suryavarman II. Walking away from the present a visitor came closer and closer to the gods.

Angkor Wat was sited in such a way that on the summer equinox (June 21), the sun would be observed rising directly behind the central tower. As the sun shifts in the course of the year, its rays illuminate a series of galleries where the bas-reliefs, in turn, depict stages in Suryavarman's life, seen in terms of the lives of Vishnu and the Indian hero Prince Rama. Other measurements inside the temple echo other Indian astronomical and religious ideas.

These complicated "readings" of Angkor Wat were thought up by priests and astronomers at Angkor, and remained unknown to scholars until the 1970's. For the priests and astronomers, the temple was a coded religious text that reflected the world of the gods. In the twelfth century, its towers were probably covered with gold leaf, and the walls were probably painted white. Many bronze and gilded statues inside the temple have disappeared, and so has the city that thrived around it. Before the collapse of Angkor in the fifteenth century, the temple must have been an extraordinary, even magical, sight, reflected in the water of the moat, and it retains much of this magic today, over eight hundred years after it was built.

Jayavarman VII

Between Suryavarman's death in 1150 and the accession of the last major Angkorean king, Jayavarman VII, thirty-one years later, Angkorean armies were at war with Champa to the east, and also with a Vietnam, then centered around what is now Hanoi. After a thousand years as part of the Chinese empire, Vietnam had recently become independent, and its armies and settlers had begun pushing south along the coast as well as westward into the mountains, putting pressure on areas until then dependent on Angkor.

Cham armies and a naval force invaded Angkor in 1177 and sacked the city. In the following year, Cham armies were defeated elsewhere in Cambodia by a Cambodian prince who came to the throne in 1181 as Jayavarman VII. Jayavarman came to power after he had spent many years in Champa, perhaps taking refuge there from Angkorean enemies, or even forming alliances with the Chams.

Jayavarman VII was a fervent Buddhist, and the last great builder-king at Angkor. He rebuilt the city's walls and redesigned the entire city, placing his own temple-mountain, the Bayon, at the center. Before building the Bayon in the 1190's, Jayavarman built two other temples honoring his parents and built or renovated over a hundred hospitals throughout the kingdom. These have disappeared, but identical inscriptions attached to sixteen of them have survived. These reveal that each of the hospitals was stocked with traditional medicines and food, staffed by over a hundred attendants. These hospitals supposedly reflected Jayavarman's caring nature:

He suffered from the illnesses of his subjects more than from his own and the evil that afflicted men's bodies became, in him, an even more piercing spiritual pain.

Some of Jayavarman's Buddhist-oriented ideas may have come from one of his wives, Indradevi, famous for her scholarly abilities. Others may have stemmed from his time in Champa, where Mahayana Buddhism was more widespread than it was at Angkor. Stone bridges constructed in Jayavarman's reign indicate that he also restored or built roads around Angkor, above the flood levels of the Tonle Sap.

Jayavarman's most important work was his reconstruction of the city of Angkor itself. New walls were flung up to enclose the city. At two of the five newly designed gates he placed rows of stone giants, perhaps representing Cambodians and Chams or Buddhists and Hindus struggling in a tug of war. Above the gates, and also on the multiple towers of the Bayon, he had carved the enormous, mysterious faces, turned in four directions, that some scholars have associated with the Buddha, others with Hindu gods, and still others with Jayavarman VII himself or with lesser guardian spirits.

What is most remarkable about the Bayon, however, are its relief sculptures of ordinary twelfth-century people engaged in everyday activities. These carvings are the earliest to give us details about the men and women who lived at Angkor, served its kings, and built its monuments. The carvings give us invaluable glimpses of material life and activities in Angkorean times. They show people at cockfights, picking fruit, bargaining at markets; ox-carts to transport rice and fish almost exactly like those in use for the same purposes today; buffalo sacrifices; parades of soldiers; court women picnicking in open boats (presumably on the Tonle Sap); dancers; and people carrying statues of Hindu gods in procession, much as they do in India today. The carvings depict a sick man being massaged; wrestlers and a juggler at a village fair; and Cham and Khmer forces in ferocious combat, on water and on land.

The Bayon is a celebration of Cambodia as well as a monument to an individual king and to the ancestors, Hindu gods, and Buddhas whom he honored. The presence of so many ordinary people in the carvings suggests that commoners, as well as the king, would earn

religious merit. Though no one can overhear the voices of these graceful, hard-working people, they move with a real sense of dignity in these fluid and expressive carvings.

Jayavarman VII is unusual in that several statues are almost certainly posed portraits of him. They depict him with his eyes half closed, in meditation. The statues were sent off to regional centers as a means of expressing Jayavarman's political control. They were probably originally placed in front of statues of the Buddha.

Jayavarman's reign was a pinnacle and a turning point in Cambodian history. Following his death, around 1220, almost no stone buildings were erected and very few Sanskrit inscriptions were carved at Angkor. All that is known about Jayavarman's successor is that he was instrumental in damaging some of the Buddha images at the Bayon and in replacing them with statues of Hindu gods.

Jayavarman VII's ambitious building program, followed by a severe reduction in building and inscriptions at Angkor, has led scholars to suggest that Jayavarman's programs had exhausted the people of Angkor, as well as the supplies of usable stone with which to build new temples. Others have suggested that the changes coincided with wars to the east and west of the kingdom, which weakened Angkor's institutions and depleted its work force.

By the mid-thirteenth century, Angkor began to experience the pressures, from what was to become Thailand and from Vietnam, that have been so characteristic of Cambodian history ever since.

This enormous deity (over ten feet high) forms part of one of the sixty towers of the Bayon. Each of the towers bears four identical faces. Scholars disagree as to whether the faces represent the Buddha, the Hindu deity Brahma, or the king who built the temple, Jayavarman VII. Note how the statue is carved in sections, which are then lowered into place. No mortar is used. A. Marc, Musée de l'Homme, Paris

Market scene, Bayon (twelfth century A.D.). The woman in the center is spinning, while the man on the left carries goods on a pole, as Cambodians do today. Notice the distended earlobes, for ivory earrings. The turtle underneath the woman spinning may have been a pet. Walter Veit

A Chinese Visitor to Angkor, 1296

The fact that the buildings ceased to be built and that Angkor was abandoned in the fifteenth century suggests that major changes must have been taking place in Cambodian society in the thirteenth and fourteenth centuries. Unfortunately, however, the shortage of documents makes it impossible for us to know what those changes were.

The changes, whatever they were, came slowly. In 1295–1296, a Chinese diplomat, Chou Ta Kuan, wrote an account of a visit to Angkor that indicates that it was still a thriving and prosperous kingdom.

His brisk, down-to-earth report is well worth reading. It is divided into forty short sections, which cover many topics. Some of these are: Birds, Agriculture, Childbirth, Clothing, Chariots, Trade, Writing, and Bathing. Although Chou was a talented observer, he tended, like most travelers, to concentrate on aspects of Angkorean life that he found strange or appealing when compared to Chinese customs. Frequent bathing, for example, he found amusing, and he was diverted by the sight of young women taking off their clothes and bathing naked in public.

Although the city had recently been attacked by Siamese (Thai) forces, it still presented a grand appearance. In Chou's words:

At the center of the kingdom rises a Golden Tower [the Bayon] flanked by more than twenty lesser towers and several hundred stone chambers. On the eastern side is a golden bridge guarded by two lions of gold, one on each side, and eight golden Buddhas spaced along the stone chambers.

Other monuments were also gilded, or covered with copper sheeting and gold leaf. At one of the temples, says Chou:

If you are looking for gold lions, gold Buddhas, bronze elephants, bronze oxen, bronze horses, here is where you will find them.

Cambodian houses were either tiled or thatched, as they are to-day, but in Angkorean times only officials were permitted to use tiles. Similarly, certain designs in cloth were reserved for high-ranking people.

Chou was fascinated with the ranking system in Cambodia and also with its religious tolerance: Buddhism, Brahmanism, and Shivaism all flourished side by side. He stayed long enough to learn some of the language, noting that officials "have their own style of speech. . . . Buddhists have their priestly jargon; and each city has its own dialect." He found this diversity "exactly the same as China." In this context, he noted that Chinese goods were much in demand, and that Chinese sailors had settled in Cambodia:

Chinese coming to the country note with pleasure that it is not necessary to wear clothes, and since rice is easily had, women easily persuaded, houses easily run . . . and trade easily carried on, a great many . . . take up permanent residence.

During his stay in Cambodia, Chou saw the Cambodian king, Indra-varman III, on four occasions. His description of a royal parade is worth quoting in detail.

When the King leaves his palace, the procession is headed by soldiers; then come the flags, the banners, the music. Girls of the palace, three to five hundred in number, with flowers in their hair and candles in their hands, are massed together in a separate column. The candles are lighted even in broad daylight. Then come other girls holding gold and silver vessels . . . of a very

Fish, a turtle, a crocodile, and a duck, crowd the water of the Tonle Sap in a bas-relief at the Bayon. Above them, warships are rowed into position.   Walter Veit

special design, and still more girls, the bodyguard of the palace, holding shields and lances. . . . Following them come chariots, adorned with gold. Ministers and princes, mounted on elephants, are preceded by bearers of scarlet umbrellas, without number. Close behind come the royal wives and concubines, on litters or chariots, or mounted on horses or elephants.

Finally the king appeared, standing erect on an elephant and holding in his hand the sacred sword. The elephant's tusks were sheathed in gold. The King was accompanied by bearers of twenty white parasols with golden shafts.

Scenes like this might have gone on for hundreds of years, and yet, less than two hundred years later, the processions, which resemble the magnificent ones carved on the walls of Angkor Wat and the Bayon, came to an end, and the city of Angkor was deserted. No one knows where the descendants of the ordinary people went. Some certainly drifted south, toward the new Cambodian capital in Phnom Penh, founded in the fifteenth century; thousands more were killed in warfare or probably were taken off as prisoners of war to Thailand and Vietnam. Little by little, the vegetation at Angkor—grass and bushes at first, and later trees—began to reclaim the landscape. Little by little, the idea of Angkor sank back into people's memories as a time when "giants" had lived in Cambodia. It was not until the French arrived in the nineteenth century that the kings of Angkor were dated and identified, and its temples labeled, as they should be, as wonders of the world.

Cambodia's Search for Independence

When Angkor was abandoned in the fifteenth century, it seems likely that many members of its elite had been shifting toward the southeast, and the vicinity of present-day Phnom Penh, for some time. This shift was partly in response to Thai pressure on Angkor, which took the form of repeated military attacks launched from a newly independent kingdom known as Ayudhya. The attacks meant that Angkor lost thousands of its people as casualties or as prisoners of war, while some of its former subjects became citizens of another kingdom.

The southward shift occurred at some point in the 1400's, but evidence suggesting why it happened is very thin. Some writers have speculated that an outbreak of malaria or some other deadly disease killed off much of Angkor's population and left the city vulnerable to attack. Others have argued that members of the Cambodian elite and Chinese merchants at Angkor found trading opportunities along the Mekong more lucrative than they had been in Angkor. By moving to the southeast they could profit from trading networks being developed elsewhere in Southeast Asia by Malay and Indian merchants. Certainly

---

Time Line

1430: Thai invasion of Angkor, the last of several, forces Cambodians to abandon it. Cambodian capital shifts southward to Phnom Penh.

1767: Thai kingdom of Ayudhya defeated by Burmese army. Chaos spreads into Cambodia from Thailand and Vietnam.

1794: New Thai regime in Bangkok places a teenaged Cambodian prince on the throne of Cambodia. He dies within three years, ushering in a period of Thai–Vietnamese conflict over Cambodia.

1841: A rebellion led by Cambodian officials against Vietnamese control brings on a Thai invasion. Six years later, Vietnamese troops withdraw; Cambodia regains its independence.

1858: Cambodian king, Duang, unsuccessfully seeks protection from the French against the Thai and Vietnamese.

1863: France proclaims a protectorate over Cambodia, concluding a treaty with Duang's son, King Norodom. Protectorate lasts until 1953.

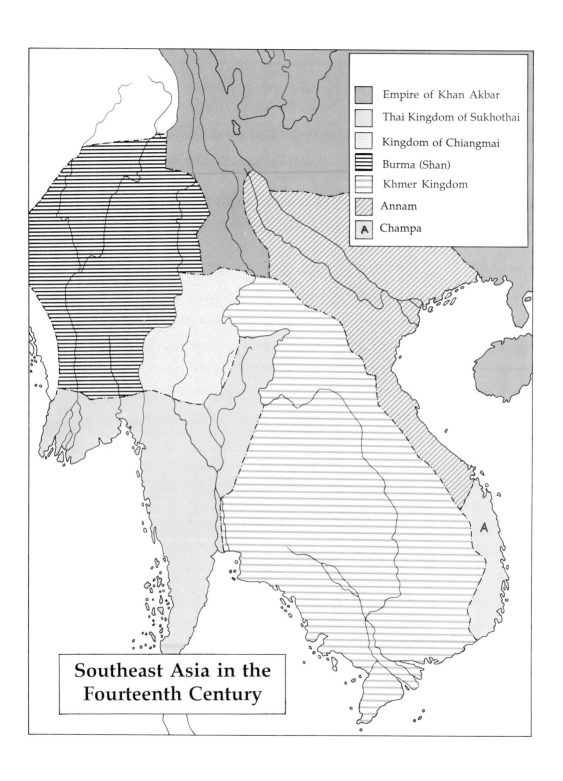

Legend

- Empire of Khan Akbar
- Thai Kingdom of Sukhothai
- Kingdom of Chiangmai
- Burma (Shan)
- Khmer Kingdom
- Annam
- A Champa

Southeast Asia in the Fourteenth Century

they were safer from attacks from the Thais in their new capital. By the late sixteenth century, Phnom Penh was a thriving international port.

Between Chou Ta Kuan's account in the 1290's and the arrival of European traders and missionaries 250 years later, documentary evidence about Cambodia is almost nonexistent. This does not mean that its civilization disappeared. Chinese records indicate that a kingdom of "Cambodia" traded with China in the fourteenth and fifteenth centuries, and Cambodia struck European visitors later on as a prosperous, cultivated place. It was even strong enough, in military terms, to launch occasional attacks of its own against the Thais.

Theravada Buddhism

Probably the most important change in Cambodia between the thirteenth and fifteenth centuries was the conversion of its people to that branch of Buddhism known as Theravada (the way of the elders), which has been the religion of nearly all Cambodians ever since.

Theravada Buddhism was established in Sri Lanka (formerly Ceylon) in the fourth century A.D.—roughly eight hundred years after the death of Gautama, known as the Buddha, or "Enlightened One."

In its early stages, Theravada Buddhism was a reform sect reacting to the animism and extravagances of Hinduism, as well as to Mahayana Buddhism, which had many Hindu features. Like the Protestants in sixteenth- and seventeenth-century Europe, who based their faith on biblical study, Theravada reformers turned to the Buddhist scriptures for their inspiration rather than to priests, rituals, or kings.

In the twelfth century, the sect spread from Sri Lanka into what is now Myanmar and then into Thailand. It soon filtered overland to Angkor, by means of Thai and Burmese merchants, artisans, and prisoners of war. By the 1290's, Chou Ta Kuan wrote of Theravada "monks

[who] shave the head, wear yellow robes, bare the right shoulder . . . and go barefoot"—just as they do today.

The monks had taken vows of poverty, celibacy, and obedience. They depended on other peoples' kindness for their food and clothing. Most Cambodian men would become monks for a time—anywhere from a few weeks to several years—before getting married and settling down. This practice persisted into the 1960's and disappeared in the Pol Pot era, when the monkhood was abolished.

In the 1290's, the Theravada monks had not been in Cambodia for long, but they were probably not impressed by Hindu rituals or by grandiose temple mountains dedicated to the divinity of kings. Instead, they preached that everything in life could be reduced to suffering and impermanence, and that only by right actions, following Buddha's teachings, could everyone in a given kingdom—rulers and slaves alike—escape the apparently endless cycle of suffering, death, and rebirth.

The monks taught that ordinary people could accumulate merit by becoming monks for a time (if they were men), leading worthy lives, and supporting the monastic order. Women gained merit, it was thought, by having sons who became monks. Naturally, kings and wealthy people could earn more merit than other people, because they had more resources at their disposal. They gained merit by such actions as erecting and decorating monasteries, supporting large numbers of monks, and freeing their personal servants. People at other levels of the society could feed monks, place their sons in monasteries, pay attention to sermons, and observe Buddhist holy days.

Theravada Buddhism did not level Cambodian society, although it

Buddhist tomb, Royal Palace, Phnom Penh. The ashes of a prince or princess are buried underneath this monument.   Charles F. Keyes

brought its kings closer to earth and offered a measure of salvation to everyone. It also diminished the importance of a hereditary priestly caste and brought everyone in touch with a clear set of religious and ethical practices.

Because of gaps in the record, it is impossible to say whether the conversion came before or after institutions at Angkor had begun to weaken. Probably the decline preceded the conversions, rather than the reverse. There is nothing in Theravada Buddhist teaching, after all, that forces its kings to be kind or warriors to be defeated. Mighty kingdoms in the region, such as seventeenth-century Ayudhya or eighteenth-century Burma, were Theravada Buddhist. The difference between Burma, Ayudhya, and fourteenth-century Angkor was not in their religions, which were identical, but in the vigor of their leaders, economies, and political institutions.

Cambodia was smaller and weaker than before, and also had new priorities. One of these was the importance it placed on trade.

Trade and Southeast Asia

In the fifteenth and sixteenth centuries, Southeast Asia experienced a sharp increase in international trade. This sprang in part from the arrival of Moslem traders from India, who converted many of the seagoing people of present-day Indonesia, the Malays, to their faith. These traders, reaching Cambodia, played an important part in changing the country from a land-based, inward looking kingdom to one that faced outward, exporting products such as gold, ivory, and spices in exchange for silk and modern weapons. Chinese traders in Cambodia maintained contact with their countrymen in the port cities of Southeast Asia, which enabled them to extend credit to each other and to trade securely over great distances long before the invention of telegraphs and telephones. Weights and measures for day-to-day trading were brought in from China and competed with local standards.

In the mid-sixteenth century, adventurers and missionaries from Portugal and Spain fanned out from their new colonies in Malacca (north of present-day Singapore) and the Philippines, seeking riches and converts to Christianity. English and Dutch traders did not appear in the region until the 1600's.

These developments meant that Cambodian rice-growing villages in the interior were no longer as closely linked, administratively, to the capital as they had been in Angkorean times, and also that the royal family itself became involved not only in trade but also, through inter-marriage, in the Chinese and Chinese-Cambodian commercial community. These trends may indeed have started in Angkorean times, where the surviving records play down the day-to-day activities of the king. They certainly lasted until the disappearance of monarchy in Cambodia in 1970.

Despite these developments, many things about Cambodia remained unchanged since Chou's visit and the Bayon bas-reliefs. A sixteenth-century Spanish missionary, for example, noted that:

All the nobles have several wives, the number depending on how rich they are. High-ranking women are white and beautiful; those of the common people are brown. These women work the soil while their husbands make war. Nobles travel in litters, which people carry on their shoulders, while the people travel by cart, on buffalo, and on horseback.

Cambodian Literature

Like most of Southeast Asia in this period, Cambodia was a vigorous, prosperous, and relatively healthy society. Indirect evidence for this is the cultural flowering of the kingdom. The most famous Cambodian classical poem, the *Reamker*—a version of the Indian *Ramayana*—was composed at this time, and so were the moral sayings known as *chbap* (laws) which until recently were memorized by Cambodian schoolchildren and formed the basis of Cambodia's ethical code.

The *chbap* offer many insights into traditional Cambodian society. They are conservative and prudent. They stress the importance of teachers, rulers, elders, and parents in molding younger people's behavior. They emphasize obedience, the importance of the past, social harmony, and the dangers of breaking with tradition. Relationships, like society itself, are not seen as equal but as lopsided, with more fortunate people protecting the poor, and the less fortunate respecting their "betters." These, in turn, protect those even further down, like children and animals. As one poem expresses it:

Take the case of a big tree
enveloped entirely by clinging vines.
The vines have asked its hospitality
so as to grow beside it.
They climb, thanks to the generosity of the tree,
they wrap themselves around it, holding on,
and produce abundant fruits and flowers.
The tree is a powerful man, the vines that depend on it, and clutch it,
are little people
who will never forget the kindness of the tree.

Everyone occupied a place that was determined by the merit earned in previous lives. Merit could be gained and increased by behaving correctly and by respecting customs. "Don't take the straight path, or the winding one," a Cambodian proverb urges. "Take the path your ancestors have taken." Another notes: "Don't confuse the raw and the

Some Cambodian Proverbs

In prerevolutionary times, proverbs played an important part, formally and informally, in Cambodian education. These well-known ones are only a few of several hundred that have been published.

If you're shy with your teacher, you'll never be wise. If you're shy with your wife, you'll never have children.

Don't believe the sky; don't believe the stars.
Don't believe your daughter when she says she has no lover.
Don't believe your mother when she says she has no debts.

The rich should take care of the poor, like a skirt that wraps the body.

Don't let an angry man wash dishes; don't let a hungry man guard rice.

If you're mean, be mean so that people respect you. If you're stupid, be stupid so that they pity you.

If a tiger lies down, don't say, "The tiger is showing respect."

If you have some tasty food, don't keep it for tomorrow. If you suspect your wife of being unfaithful, don't let her walk behind you.

cooked; everything is regulated by law. No cleverness can ever overturn wise rules set out in distant times."

Missionaries and Cambodia

In the mid-sixteenth century, Spanish and Portuguese missionaries came to Cambodia, hoping to convert local people to Christianity and even to join Cambodia to the Spanish Empire. They had some success with minority populations, but little among the Buddhist Khmer. As one missionary commented, "Christians cannot be made without the king's approval." He went on to say that "the common people" worshipped the Buddhist monks:

There is no person who dares contradict them in anything. [It] happened that while I was preaching, many round me hearing me very well, and being very satisfied with what I told them, that if there come along any of these priests and said, "This is good but ours is better," they would all depart.

The Cambodian kings tolerated the missionaries without encouraging them, because they hoped to gain benefits for themselves by trading with the new European settlements. Goods in demand from Cambodia and Laos included ivory, gold, incense, lacquer, spices, hides, precious stones, and rhinoceros horns. At this stage Moslem advisors, probably Cham converts or Malays, appeared at the Cambodian court. International trading was largely in their hands. The Cambodian words *kompong* (port) and *psaa* (market) come from Malay. Phnom Penh at this time was cosmopolitan, with Japanese, Malay, European, and Arab sections of the city.

Rediscovering Angkor

In the 1550's a Cambodian king, hunting for rhinoceros near Angkor, rediscovered the deserted temples, marveled at their sturdiness and

Cambodian silk (c. 1920) depicts European sailing ships, perhaps seventeenth century, outside a palace guarded by white elephants, thought to be semidivine in many Buddhist countries. The tie-dye technique of silk weaving, which is very time-consuming, is one Cambodia shares with Malaysia and Indonesia. Musée de l'Homme, Paris beauty, and set up court in Angkor Thom for a few years. A Portuguese missionary, de Couto, has left a valuable account of Angkor's appearance at this time. He wrote of Angkor Wat that "it was of such a strange construction that it would be impossible to describe it in writing, or compare it with any other building in the world." Later Spanish writers suggested that the temples had been built by the Lost Tribes of Israel, or the ancient Greeks!

The king used "several thousand" workers over a short period to burn and clear underbrush from the temples. Soon the temple had become a Buddhist shrine. Inscriptions from Angkor Wat commemorate activities by high-ranking Khmer officials in the 1560's and 1570's. Other inscriptions from the seventeenth and eighteenth centuries show that it was visited by people anxious to make merit for themselves. The use of Angkor Wat as a Buddhist shrine, with a monastery attached, persisted into the twentieth century. By the 1570's, however, the king and his courtiers had returned to Lovek, about forty miles (about 64 kilometers) north of Phnom Penh.

Wars with Siam

One reason for the move was that they felt safer in Lovek than at Angkor from Thai attacks. In the 1580's, Cambodian kings, capitalizing on a recent Burmese victory over Siam (now Thailand), launched attacks themselves along the Siamese–Cambodian border, hoping to round up prisoners of war and to reassert control over Khmer-speaking parts of Siam. Such attacks were ill-advised, not only because the Thai were stronger, but because when a Cambodian army, led by the king and his best generals, was absent from the capital, dissident officials and princes often plotted to steal the throne. Sooner or later Cambodian attacks produced a more powerful Thai response. The long-term effect of this adventurism was to place the Khmer court under the Thai shadow for nearly five hundred years.

Fear of Siam, dynastic instability, and exaggerated confidence in European technology (cannons came into use in Southeast Asia at about this time) led a Cambodian king in the 1590's to plead with Spanish authorities in Manila for military help, offering Catholic missionaries freedom to work in Cambodia in exchange. Soon afterward, two Spanish soldiers of fortune, who had walked into Cambodia from Vietnam, offered their services to the king just as a Thai army was besieging Lovek. The king sent them back to Manila for reinforcements; by the time they reached Phnom Penh, several months later, the capital had fallen, a Thai garrison occupied it, and their patron, the former Cambodian king, had fled northward into Laos. Soon afterward, the two Spaniards were killed in Phnom Penh.

The story reveals the ease with which visitors, from "outer space" as it were, could gain the confidence of the king, whose contacts with the outside world were few and who was convinced of his own importance. It also shows how courageous, ruthless armed intruders from the West could bewilder and dominate peasant societies—an ability that the Spaniards had already displayed in their conquest of America and the Philippines.

Cambodia in 1600

The Thai capture of Lovek in 1597 marked the end of Cambodia's independence. Cambodia's court regalia were removed, and libraries and archives were destroyed. A widespread Cambodian legend, supposedly about the fall of Lovek, explains the country's perennial weakness by the fact that statues of a sacred cow and the Buddha had been taken away by the Thai armies at this time. According to the legend, the statue of the cow had served as a container for magic documents, known as *kbuon*, written on strips of gold foil. These made those who owned them, it was thought, all-powerful, and the Thai "were able to take the books . . . and study their contents. For this reason they have become superior in knowledge to the Cambodians, and for this reason the Cambodians remain ignorant."

Even in the 1970's, high-ranking Cambodian army officers would use the legend to explain why Cambodian armies fought less well than foreigners such as Thai or Vietnamese. They had literally been deprived of the military and cultural skills that had made early Cambodia a great power.

By the beginning of the seventeenth century, Cambodia had become a satellite of Siam. Thai ceremonies were imposed on the court, Cambodian soldiers were recruited to fight in Siamese wars, and many Thai words and expressions entered the Khmer language.

Cambodian rulers who were unhappy with this, or dissatisfied princes eager to gain power, sometimes sought alliances with Cambodia's neighbors to the east, the Vietnamese, who were gradually moving into Cambodian-speaking areas of the Mekong Delta, in what is now Vietnam. In exchange for these alliances, the Vietnamese rulers of the south, the Nguyen clan, obtained administrative control over many of these areas. The sleepy Cambodian port of Prey Nokor (Forest City) at the mouth of the Mekong was taken over in this way in the 1620's and renamed Saigon (it is now known as Ho Chi Minh City, and houses several million people). Soon afterward, smaller ports along the Gulf of Thailand were occupied by Chinese traders and Vietnamese troops. By about 1700, Cambodia was cut off from the maritime world of Southeast Asia and from Europeans too. This isolation lasted for almost two hundred years.

The history of the next century is made up of repeated invasions from Vietnam and Siam, preceded and followed by ruinous civil wars. These were conducted against a background of court intrigue, violence, and uncertainty that contrasts sharply with the sedate, elegant values of the *chbap*, or the slow, intricate movements of Cambodian classical dance, which was probably perfected at this time. Most of these conflicts ignited when rival princes sought foreign help to press their claims to power. It is likely that during this tumultuous century, Cambodia lost tens of thousands of people as casualties or as prisoners of war. It never regained the strength it had enjoyed in the 1600's.

Those parts of Cambodia most affected by these disturbances were those that lay along the traditional invasion routes from the northwest and southeast respectively. In other parts of the country, many Cambodians went about the business of growing food, raising families, and observing Buddhist rules.

Cambodian Folktales

Cambodian folktales, which survived these troubling periods, have few militant or powerful heroes. Instead, they show how clever animals—particularly monkeys and hares—can outwit slower, more powerful ones like elephants and crocodiles. They depict peasant men and women outwitting their husbands, wives, fathers-in-law, Chinese merchants, nobles, and others in authority. In the tales, wily adventurers—Tmenh Chey is the most famous of these—survive hardship and humiliation by using their wits. Like many Cambodians today, the stories are endowed with an indomitable humor. The stories point out the weaknesses of the powerful and the virtues of downtrodden animals and people. They demonstrate the importance above all of surviving with one's sense of humor and one's values intact.

Wars with Siam and Vietnam

Cambodians needed more than resilience to survive onslaughts by the Thai and Vietnamese. Both countries, from the 1770's onward, were

engulfed in dynastic crises. In Siam, these followed the capture of Ayudhya by Burmese forces in 1767. In Vietnam, the Tay Son rebellion sought to overthrow the ruling dynasty of northern Vietnam and establish a dynasty, based in the center of the country around Hue (pronounced "whey") with what were for the period revolutionary ideas of equality and social justice.

The Tay Son rebellion spilled into Cambodia in the 1780's, and so did Thai armies, seeking to capitalize on instability in southern Vietnam and to display the might of the new Thai monarch, Taksin, who had seized the throne in the aftermath of Ayudhya's collapse. The Cambodian monarch brashly refused to send tribute to Taksin, on the grounds that he was half Chinese and had no royal blood. To avenge this insult, Taksin sent his minister of war at the head of an invading army. Cambodian forces were defeated. The minister overthrew Taksin himself in 1782, and became the first king in the dynasty that has held power in Bangkok ever since.

By the early 1790's, therefore, Cambodia had been marched across, and laid waste, by many foreign armies. Its legitimate ruler was a teenaged prince, held hostage by the Thai court in Bangkok. "Cambodia," without a monarch, momentarily disappeared, but came back to life in 1794, when the Thai agreed to crown their young hostage, Prince Eng, and send him back to rule from the Cambodian capital of Udong, north of Phnom Penh. His descendants held the throne until 1970, when his great-great-grandson, Prince Norodom Sihanouk, was overthrown.

Top left: Illustration from a Cambodian folktale. Here a victorious princess supervises the dismemberment of a rival, who has already been beheaded. H. Roger-Viollet

Bottom left: A demon-crocodile attacks a ship. A princely passenger prepares to fight. Illustration from a nineteenth-century Cambodian folktale. H. Roger-Viollet

A New Dynasty: The "Two-Headed Bird"

In exchange for placing Eng on the throne, the Thai took over the northwestern quarter of Cambodia, comprising the rich province of Battambang and the poorer one of Siem Reap, which contained the Angkorean ruins. The Khmer regained both provinces, with French help, in 1907.

Eng ruled for three years. When he died, his eldest son, Prince Chan, was still a minor, and a semiprisoner of the Thai. Chan fretted at this relationship, and soon entered into secret negotiations with the newly established Nguyen dynasty in Vietnam, seeking their protection. By 1810, soon after Chan had been crowned by his Thai patrons, Cambodia became a satellite of both Vietnam and Siam—a "two-headed bird," as a chronicle called it, facing both east and west. Chan hoped that the Vietnamese would protect him against the Thai. His brothers, taken off to Bangkok by a Thai army in 1811, were held in reserve in Bangkok. For twenty years, Thai, Cambodian, and Vietnamese forces skirmished in Cambodia without gaining an advantage. Chan was more or less a prisoner in his palace, watched over by Vietnamese counselors and isolated from his subjects. In the 1830's, a full-scale Thai invasion failed, and to prevent a repetition, the Vietnamese established a thorough-going system of political control that lasted until they were driven out of Cambodia by another Thai army in 1848. During this period, the Vietnamese named one of Chan's daughters (he had no sons) as "Queen" of Cambodia, but kept her locked in her palace.

Faced with a choice of domination by one power or the other, most nineteenth-century Cambodians would probably have preferred the Thai, who were culturally similar to themselves and less demanding in peacetime than the Vietnamese. The Thai expected the Cambodian king to respect them and to send them tribute, but left him free to appoint his own officials and govern Cambodia in his own way. The Vietnamese imitated a Chinese model. They put their own officials into Cambodia, made Khmer officials learn Vietnamese, and asked them to bow in the direction of the distant Vietnamese emperor twice a month. To the Vietnamese, this process amounted to civilizing the Khmer, whom they considered to be barbarians.

Vietnamese behavior angered many Cambodian officials, who had been accustomed to governing their provinces in their own way. The Vietnamese were driven out following a Cambodian revolt, whose leaders called on military help from Bangkok.

In 1848, Chan's youngest brother, Duang, by then a middle-aged man, came to the Cambodian throne. He had been in exile in Siam for most of his life, and Cambodia had been almost constantly at war. For the exhausted Khmer, peace was welcome. In the next ten years, Cambodia slowly came back to life as monasteries were rebuilt and royal ceremonies were renewed; people were again allowed to raise their children and grow their crops. To many, Duang seemed a kind of savior: An inscription from 1851 speaks of his "merit, skill, and masterly intelligence." Although Duang was careful to stay on good terms with his patron, the Thai king, he was welcomed by his own officials after their eclipse under the Vietnamese. A recognizable kingdom gradually took shape.

Duang's Reign

During Duang's reign, French forces had landed in southern Vietnam to avenge the executions of several missionaries there. By 1860, when Duang died, they had established a colony centered on Saigon. As they settled down, the new colonists turned curious eyes to the west, where Cambodia was in the midst of a civil war. A French explorer, Henri

A Vietnamese Emperor
and Cambodia (1838)

Vietnamese Emperor Minh Mang (reigned 1820–1840) supervised the Vietnamese occupation of Cambodia in the 1830's. In these two passages he laments the inefficiency of the Khmer and asks his viceroy in Cambodia to "civilize" the Khmer with Vietnamese customs and advice.

We have tried to punish and reward Cambodian officials according to their merits or demerits. We have asked the king to help us, but he has hesitated to do so. After studying the situation, we have decided that Cambodian officials only know how to bribe and be bribed. Offices are sold; nobody carries out orders; everyone works for his own account. When we tried to recruit soldiers, the king was perfectly willing, but the officials concealed great numbers of people. When we wanted to compile a list of meritorious officials, [the officials were willing, but]

Mouhot, had "discovered" the Angkorean ruins in 1859 (tipped off by a less flamboyant missionary who had been guided to them by Khmer in the 1840's). The "lost city" included a Buddhist monastery with nearly a thousand resident monks.

Spurred on by these discoveries, the French were eager to expand into Cambodia, which they were convinced was rich in minerals and provided a back door to China.

Duang's eldest son, Prince Norodom, was in a relatively weak position, patronized by the Thai court and unable to suppress uprisings led the king was unwilling, because he was jealous. For the last four months, nothing has been accomplished.

> . . . *The barbarians in Cambodia have become my children now, and you [i.e. the Vietnamese viceroy] should help them, and teach them our customs. . . . I have heard for example that the land is fertile, and that there are plenty of oxen [for plowing] . . . but the people use picks and hoes, instead of oxen. They grow enough rice for two meals a day, but they don't store any surplus. Daily necessities like pork, silk, and ducks are very expensive. Now all these shortcomings stem from the laziness of the Cambodians, and my instructions to you are these: teach them to raise mulberry trees [to feed silkworms], pigs, and ducks. . . . As for language, they should be taught to speak Vietnamese. If there is any outdated or barbarous custom that can be simplified or repressed, then do so. . . . Let the good ideas seep in, turning barbarians into civilized people.*

Three years later, Cambodians revolted against Vietnamese control.

by one of his brothers and other pretenders to the throne. The Thai court, uncertain of his loyalty, delayed offering him his crown, which was in safe-keeping in Bangkok. In 1863, he agreed to accept French "protection" of his kingdom, hoping to use this as a counterweight to Thai control and as a means of obtaining military help. In a way, he was trying to preserve his independence. Instead, he opened the door onto nearly a century of French colonial domination.

From Colonialism to Independence

Early Stages of Colonialism

When a handful of French naval officers sent up from Saigon established a protectorate over Cambodia in 1863, they had no long-term policies, and no idea how long France would stay. They had come into Cambodia because no other European power had claimed it, because they imagined that it was richer than it was, and to protect their new colony in southern Vietnam. They took possession of the country because it was easy to do so. They also felt that French influence over its "primitive" people and institutions would be beneficial.

The French established themselves in Cambodia soon after they had set up a protectorate over several provinces in southern Vietnam. They renamed the provinces Cochin China. Over the rest of the nineteenth century, the French extended their control, by diplomatic and military means, over the remainder of Vietnam. They added the Lao states on the upper Mekong to their empire in the early 1900's. French efforts were matched by the British intrusion into Burma and Malaysia in the 1880's, the American annexation of the Philippines from Spain in 1898, and the gradual expansion of the Dutch empire from its bases in Java and Sumatra into all the islands of present-day Indonesia. Cambodia's colonial era was one in which European powers and the United States took control of the rest of Southeast Asia. Only Siam (which changed its name to Thailand in 1939) remained an independent state.

The French stayed on for ninety years, protecting Cambodians from other European powers, from the Thai, and from the perils of independence. The protectorate form of governing the country meant that its kings continued in office, although those after Norodom were specifically selected by the French. Similarly, Cambodian officials, such as provincial governors and tax-collectors, worked alongside the French instead of losing their positions. Kingship and other institutions were frozen in place for nearly a hundred years. For the first twenty years of their protectorate, the French did little to interfere with traditional politics.

Time Line

1884–1886: Cambodians revolt against French rule. Rebellion put down by Norodom's brother, Sisowath, who cooperates with the French.

1904: On Norodom's death, the French name Sisowath king. He rules until 1927, presides over economic growth.

1927: Sisowath succeeded by his son, Monivong.

1941: Japanese forces occupy Cambodia with consent of French authorities, who remain in day-to-day control. Monivong dies and is succeeded by his grandson, Norodom Sihanouk, then only nineteen years old.

1945: Japanese imprison French authorities, give Cambodia its independence. At war's end, French renew their protectorate.

1946–1953: Political parties flourish in Cambodia. French gradually withdraw, under pressure from Communist guerrillas and later from King Sihanouk.

1955: Sihanouk abdicates the throne, starts a political movement that gains all the seats in the National Assembly.

1955–1970: Sihanouk rules Cambodia almost single-handedly. Expands education, pursues neutralist foreign policy to avoid entanglement with Thailand and South Vietnam.

1960: Communist Party of Cambodia founded. Three years later, it comes under the leadership of Saloth Sar, who later takes revolutionary name of Pol Pot.

1963: Sihanouk breaks off economic relations with the United States.

1966–1967: Communist insurgency in Cambodia forces Sihanouk to counter by installing pro-American government. In South Vietnam, war between United States and its anti-Communist allies against North Vietnam and South Vietnamese Communists expands.

1969: U.S. planes, with Sihanouk's secret approval, bomb Vietnamese supply lines inside Cambodia.

1970: Sihanouk overthrown, while overseas, by his own cabinet. Vowing revenge, Sihanouk takes command of Cambodian Communist forces pledged to overthrow new government, which is allied with United States.

1975: Communist forces capture Phnom Penh, control Cambodia, evacuate the cities, and inaugurate a far-reaching revolutionary program throughout the country.

1976–1978: Democratic Kampuchea (D.K.), the new Communist government in Cambodia, presides over at least a million deaths among Cambodians from starvation, overwork, diseases, and executions.

1977: D.K. forces conduct brutal raids into Communist Vietnam. Cambodian Communist Party purges many of its members, accusing them of working for the Vietnamese. China supports Democratic Kampuchea.

1979: Vietnamese Communist army invades Cambodia and places a pro-Vietnamese government in power in Phnom Penh. Pol Pot and other D.K. figures flee to Thailand.

1981: Pol Pot, Sihanouk, and a former Cambodian prime minister, Son Sann, form a coalition government in exile that gains recognition from the United Nations. U.S.S.R., Soviet bloc, and India recognize Cambodian Vietnamese-sponsored government in Phnom Penh.

1981–1989: Diplomatic isolation of Cambodia prevents its economic development, while Vietnamese military forces in Cambodia prevent Democratic Kampuchea and coalition from regaining power. People's Republic of Kampuchea, founded by Vietnamese, gains domestic confidence and popularity.

1989: P.R.K. changes its name to State of Cambodia. Vietnamese withdraw their troops from Cambodia. Civil war breaks out soon afterward along Thai frontier.

1990: Several international conferences convened to seek peace in Cambodia.

When he signed the treaty with the French, King Norodom probably had no idea what he was getting into, and he managed to keep his treaty a secret from his Thai advisors for several months. When they found out about it and notified Bangkok, he reversed himself and declared that he wanted to "remain the servant of [the Thai king] until the end [of his] life."

French diplomatic pressure on Bangkok forced the Thai to back off. To save face, the Thai agreed to "cooperate" with the French in celebrating Norodom's coronation. By the end of the 1860's Norodom's Thai advisors had gone home. Thai influence at his court, and elsewhere in Cambodia, had ended.

By then, at French insistence, Norodom had moved his capital from Udong to Phnom Penh, which was accessible from Saigon and harder to reach from Siam. It was also, even then, a largely Chinese commercial city, rather than merely a palace surrounded by villages, as Udong and other Cambodian capitals had been.

The Mekong Expedition

In the late 1860's, French explorers traveled up the Mekong and found that its sources lay in the inhospitable mountains of western China. Large stretches of the river were not navigable for ocean-going ships. Others by then had found that Cambodia was rich in agricultural products, but without many mineral resources. These discoveries meant that Cambodia was neither a "back door" nor a source of riches for the French, and in commercial terms, the colonists lost interest. In the 1870's and 1880's, they turned their attention to conquering other parts of Indochina. Ironically, Cambodia owed its independence from the Thai to the fact that it was now linked closely to a culturally different, recently domineering state (Vietnam) as well as to a smaller, less-developed one to which Cambodians had seldom paid much attention (Laos). Most Cambodians preferred to think of their country as a kind of island, and resented being tied formally to Laos and Vietnam.

Despite Cambodia's failure as a commercial enterprise, the 1860's and 1870's were heroic years for many French administrators and explorers. The kingdom was at peace, and local officials left little for French administrators to do. These young men were not interested in administration. Throughout this period, the French in charge of Cambodia were naval officers. Many of them such as Francis Garnier, Louis Delaporte, and Jean Moura, possessed great energy, curiosity, and sympathy for the Khmer. They explored the Mekong, learned Cambodian, deciphered Angkorean inscriptions, and arranged for shipments of tons of Cambodian sculpture to museums overseas. In the early twentieth century, the French built a museum for Angkorean art in Phnom Penh. Its magnificent collection of sculpture and bronzeware survived the tumultuous 1970's more or less intact.

For these young naval officers, crisscrossing the country on horseback, on elephants, and in canoes, it was exhilarating and romantic to come across stone and brick temples, Hindu statuary, and Sanskrit inscriptions; evidence of a "lost" civilization that had flourished, unnoticed by the West, during the European Middle Ages. The grandeur that they found contrasted sharply with what they considered to be the "decay" of Norodom's court and the "helplessness" of the rural Khmer.

Cambodia in the 1870's

And yet there was probably little difference, aside from scale, between the way that rural Cambodia was governed in the 1860's and the way Angkor had been governed a thousand years before. Government meant a network of relationships, graded on an upward scale from farmers to

Rediscovering Angkor (1860)

In early 1860, a French naturalist, Henri Mouhot (1826–1861), visited Angkor and spent three weeks among the ruins. His diary, published in 1864, aroused wide interest in France, which had just laid claim to Cambodia. Mouhot believed the monuments to be more than two thousand years old. He wrote:

There are ruins of such grandeur, remains of structures that must have been raised at such an immense cost of labor that . . . one is filled with profound admiration, and cannot but ask what has become of this powerful race, so civilized, so enlightened, the authors of these gigantic works?

One of these temples [Angkor Wat] might take an honorable place beside our most beautiful buildings. It is grander than anything left to us by Greece or Rome, and presents a sad contrast to the barbarism in

the king. Farmers paid officials with rice, forest products, or labor. Officials passed on some of these payments to the king, who used them to decorate his palace, feed his wives and followers, and sponsor religious festivals to make merit. Officials were never accountable to anyone lower down. Theoretically, the king's power was absolute. In practice, Cambodia had no standing army, and Norodom was hemmed in by hostile relatives, suspicious provincial chieftains, and, increasingly, by the French.

The traditional system worked because no alternative had ever been imagined. Nothing bound officials together except their own self-interest. When a king was unpopular, as Norodom was, there were frequent rebellions against his rule.

In the 1880's, the French tightened their controls on Indochina. In *which [Cambodia] is now plunged. . . . All this region is now as lonely and deserted as formerly it must have been full of life and cheerfulness; and the howling of wild animals, and the cries of a few birds, alone disturb the solitude.*

Sad fragility of human things! How many centuries and thousands of generations have passed away, of which history, probably, will never tell us anything; what riches and treasures will remain buried forever beneath these ruins?

. . . I have written these few notes on Cambodia, by the light of a torch, seated on my tiger skin. On one side of me is the skin of an ape, just stripped off; on the other, a box of insects waiting to be arranged and packed. . . . My desire is not to impose my opinions on anyone, but simply to disclose the existence of these monuments, which are certainly more gigantic, and to my mind display more perfect taste, than any left to us by [Egypt, Greece, or Rome].

Cambodia, they sought to collect more taxes, to abolish unpaid labor, and to transform the king's theoretically unlimited income into a fixed allowance.

The 1885 Rebellion

Norodom signed the new treaty setting forth these provisions in 1884, when a French official visited him and a French gunboat on the Mekong trained its cannons on his palace. A rebellion broke out in the countryside almost at once and dragged on for the next two years. Local officials correctly saw the French reforms as an attack on their traditional powers, which were based on the control of people rather than land. Their "slaves," in turn, were frightened by the possibility of change, and joined their patrons to fight the French.

The rebellion spread rapidly through the eastern part of Cambodia and required several thousand French soldiers to put down. The rebels, sheltered by sympathetic villagers, employed hit-and-run tactics and took advantage of their knowledge of waterways and terrain. The slow progress of the French revealed how a guerrilla force, supported by the people, could hold a better-trained and better-equipped colonial army at bay. Fighting stopped only when the French modified their political demands.

Even before the rebellion, the French had begun to favor Norodom's younger brother, Sisowath, and had secretly promised him the throne if Norodom rejected their reforms. Sisowath helped the French subdue the rebels in 1884–1886 but had to wait until Norodom's death in 1904 before becoming king. During these years, rivalries developed between

Prince Sisowath, King Norodom's brother, borne on a litter in southern Cambodia, 1866. Prince Sisowath was a favorite of the French and was king of Cambodia from 1904 to 1927. Bibliothèque Nationale, Paris, courtesy of Jacques Nepote

the so-called "Norodom" and "Sisowath" branches of the royal family. Some of these animosities lasted into the 1960's and beyond.

During Norodom's final years, the French limited his power and at one point tried to dethrone him on the made-up grounds that he was insane. By the 1890's they paid little attention to him or his advisors. Instead, they appointed regional officials, planned Cambodia's budget, and collected taxes themselves. Cambodia became a colony in all but name.

Sisowath's Reign (1904–1927)

Sisowath was sixty-four when his brother died. He reigned placidly until his death in 1927, sustained by his addiction to opium, his Buddhist piety, and the gilded palace constructed for him on the banks of the Mekong by the French.

Two developments are of interest from his reign. The first was the recovery of the northwestern provinces of Battambang and Siem Reap in 1907. The second was the economic boom that affected most of Indochina in the 1920's.

By 1907, French scholars had deciphered hundreds of Angkorean inscriptions in Sanskrit and Khmer. Sisowath and educated Cambodians, particularly in the Buddhist monkhood, became aware that Angkor had not been built by gods or giants, as some of them had thought, but by their own ancestors. It was humiliating that the temples were under Thai control. To avoid war with France, the Thai agreed to give the provinces back to Cambodia. Sisowath was overjoyed, and traveled soon afterward to Angkor for ceremonies of thanksgiving.

Developments in the 1920's

During the 1920's, as Sisowath drifted into old age (he had been born in 1840), Cambodia shared in the economic boom that affected the rest of Indochina. Thousands of miles of roads, and a 500-mile (800-kilometer) railroad, were planned and built before 1930. Phnom Penh was modernized and electrified, taking on the appearance of a French provincial town. Beginning in 1918, thousands of acres were planted with rubber trees in eastern and northeastern Cambodia, often adjoining similar plantations in southern Vietnam. By 1930, these plantations, owned by French companies, produced some of the highest quality rubber in the world. In the northwest, rice production was stimulated by the development of export markets and improved transportation systems.

A byproduct of the boom was that tens of thousands of Vietnamese migrated into Cambodia to work on the plantations and in small industry and to fill the lower ranks of the civil service. Because the educational system in Cochin China was more evolved than its Cambodian counterpart, more Vietnamese than Cambodians could read French. This skill made them useful to the French, and many Cambodians, forced to deal with the Vietnamese when paying taxes, for example, came to resent their privileged status.

Few benefits from the economic boom of the 1920's flowed out to rural people, whose high taxes went to pay bureaucrats' salaries and to finance roads, administrative buildings, and other public works that benefited the French. Colonial investments in education, public health, and sanitation, on the other hand, were small. By 1940, Cambodia had only three trained doctors, one hospital, and a single high school to serve its three million people.

The French considered Cambodia to be an enchanted, sleepy place and did almost nothing to aid its people. The new King, Sisowath Monivong (reigned 1927–1941), had been hand picked by the French. During his years in power, he supervised productions of royal classical dance, translated *The Arabian Nights* from French into Khmer, smoked opium, and watched benignly as the 1920's and then the 1930's rolled past the open windows of the palace. One of his many wives, the daughter of rich peasants in Kompong Thom, was the sister of Saloth Sar (Pol Pot), who in the 1970's became the prime minister of the Communist government in Phnom Penh.

Early Nationalism

Under Monivong, the first Cambodian-language newspaper, named after Angkor Wat, appeared, and was widely read by bureaucrats and in the monastic order. In the meantime, more and more Cambodians, although still only a few hundred in all, gained high-school educations. Little by little, a Cambodian elite separate from the royal family and the Chinese merchant class, but still concentrated in Phnom Penh, was taking shape.

When World War II broke out in Europe in 1939, Indochina was cut off from France, a situation that got worse when France surrendered to the Germans in 1940. Japanese forces at war in China had been pressing against the northern frontier of Vietnam. In 1941, with French permission, several thousand Japanese troops came to be stationed in Cambodia, Laos, and Vietnam. Soon afterward, Thai armies attacked Cambodia, hoping to capitalize on French military weakness to regain the "lost" provinces of Battambang and Siem Reap.

Defeated on land, the French defeated the Thai navy at sea, and Japan stepped in to negotiate between the two sides. Battambang was given back to Thailand, but the French retained possession of Angkor. King Monivong, angered at the French failure to defend his kingdom, ceased speaking French (the administrative language of Cambodia) and retired to his model farm, emotionally broken. He died soon afterward, aged 66.

King Norodom Sihanouk

His eldest son, Prince Sisowath Monireth (1909–1975), expected to be crowned, but the French were reluctant to agree, because they felt that the Prince's strong character, good education, and administrative skills might impede their policies, especially in the delicate political situation imposed by World War II. Instead, in 1941 they chose Monireth's nephew, the nineteen-year-old Norodom Sihanouk, then a high-school student in Saigon. The French thought that Sihanouk—a quiet, sensitive boy, gifted at music and interested in movies—would be a more suitable ruler than his strongminded uncle. Moreover, they hoped to appease the Norodom and Sisowath branches by choosing a monarch descended, as the young king was, from both of the two brothers.

For the next four years Sihanouk was a pliable, cooperative king. To counter Japanese propaganda, the French encouraged him to travel around his kingdom and elsewhere in Indochina. Everywhere he went, in Cambodia at least, people greeted him reverently on their knees, their eyes averted from his glance. While in one sense he was a creature of the colonial powers, Sihanouk noticed that he was thought of as a religious object or a god by many ordinary Khmer.

Cambodia's First Independence

In March 1945, the Japanese forces in Indochina, fearing an Allied invasion, arrested French officials and told the rulers of Laos, Cambodia, and Vietnam that their countries were independent. For the next seven months, the "Kingdom of Kampuchea," as it was called, went through the motions of being free from colonial rule. A nationalist leader, Son Ngoc Thanh, returned from exile in Tokyo and became prime minister. King Sihanouk, taking advice from new advisors, made rousing patriotic speeches. In the countryside, with the police in jail, many Cambodians became bandits, and others armed themselves to resist the French when they returned to power.

The Kingdom of Kampuchea lasted until October 1945, a month after Japan's surrender. The French came back in force, imprisoned Son Ngoc Thanh, and wrote a speech for Sihanouk to deliver welcoming their return.

Bowing to circumstances once again, Sihanouk resumed his role as a puppet of the French. He attended French army cavalry training in France, agreed to a constitution that limited his powers, and busied himself with horseback riding, composing popular music, and making movies.

Politics after World War II

In the meantime, the French had permitted political parties to flourish in Cambodia, while refusing to give up political and economic power. The most important party, the Democrats, won elections in 1946, 1947, and 1951. The French found the Democrats' pro-independence policies offensive, and Sihanouk sensed that many of them wanted to turn the country into a republic rather than a monarchy. With French help, he dissolved the National Assembly in 1952, scattered the Democrats, and started ruling by decree.

At this point, with the opposition removed, Sihanouk began to see himself as Cambodia's best political leader. He embarked on what he called a "Royal Crusade for Independence," putting pressure on the French to withdraw from Cambodia. The Crusade, which the king took to several foreign countries, was gratifying to Sihanouk and humiliating to the French. In November 1953, they reluctantly agreed to grant Cambodia independence, ahead of Laos and Vietnam. Sihanouk, triumphant, was declared a National Hero soon afterward in a decree he signed himself.

Sihanouk had waited to oppose the French until he thought he had a chance to win. Since 1945, however, resistance forces in the countryside, gradually dominated by the Indochina Communist Party and the Vietnamese, had bravely confronted the French in Cambodia, killing hundreds of French soldiers and losing hundreds of their own. Casualties were far lower than in Vietnam but were sufficient to pin down sizeable bodies of French troops inside Cambodia. Without this pressure it is doubtful that the French would have given in to Sihanouk's demands. This period of struggle throughout the region, which lasted from 1946 to 1954, is often called the First Indochina War.

Many young Cambodians in the 1940's and early 1950's were drawn toward the resistance, which, unlike the king, offered the exciting possibility of revolutionary social change. Some of the better educated, pursuing college courses in France, were persuaded to become Communists. This generation (born for the most part in the late 1920's and early 1930's) was impressed by the dedication of the French and Vietnamese Communists they met and admired the successful rise to power of Communists under Mao Zedong in China. Cambodian radicals in France included Pol Pot, Ieng Sary, and Son Sen, among others, who later became important figures in Democratic Kampuchea.

Pol Pot returned from France in early 1953 and joined the Communist-led resistance forces, dominated by the Vietnamese, for several months. During his time in France, he had been aided financially by his older brother, who worked in Sihanouk's palace. But Pol Pot's time in France had made him an opponent of royalty and a believer in violent resistance. Under communism, he thought, Cambodian hierarchies would dissolve, and everyone would be equal. Leaders would not be kings, princes, and corrupt officials but intelligent, dedicated members of the Party, like himself. In the process, Cambodia would be transformed.

The Elections of 1955

The rest of Indochina became independent in 1954, following an international conference in Geneva, Switzerland. The conference decided that the Indochinese states should conduct elections to determine who should rule. For Sihanouk, this meant that the Democrats might return to power; for Pol Pot and his friends, working in secret in Phnom Penh, the elections were an opportunity to bring some Communist sympathizers into the Assembly.

In 1955, Sihanouk made another of the dramatic, unpredicted moves that characterized his long career. Without any warning, he gave up the throne, naming his father king, and inaugurated a national political movement, known as Sangkum Reastr Niyum (People's Socialist Community), that was intended to replace existing political parties. Its "nonpolitical" leader was Sihanouk himself.

Sihanouk's move capitalized on his deep and widespread popularity. Many Cambodians believed that he was the father of Cambodian independence. Many more, perhaps, considered him semidivine, and felt it was their duty to vote as he demanded.

In the Assembly elections in September 1955, the Sangkum won all the seats, officially, although a more honest election might have resulted in half a dozen seats going to the opposing political parties. In any event, the political parties soon disappeared, and Sihanouk interpreted the vote, correctly, as a mandate to govern Cambodia single-handedly. For the next fifteen years—as Prime Minister, Father of Independence, and Chief of State—he never looked back.

From Independence to Revolution

From 1955 to 1970, Norodom Sihanouk dominated nearly every aspect of Cambodian life. As *samdech euv* (prince papa), the self-proclaimed father of his people, he toured the kingdom tirelessly, delivering three- and four-hour speeches at top speed and sometimes, when he was angry, at the top of his voice. In these talks, delivered in slangy, colloquial Khmer, the prince made fun of his opponents and foreigners, while praising his "children," Angkor, and the achievements of the Sangkum, his national political movement. The speeches were rebroadcast several times, but only became "official" when they were translated into French (with the jokes left out) and printed in the nation's press.

Sihanouk also dominated the media, cabinet meetings, and Cambodia's relations with foreign countries. Any documents from this period are filled with Sihanouk's voice, with his photographs, and with accounts of his achievements.

Everything he did reflected his theatrical skills. Sometimes he would hover above a village in a helicopter, tossing bolts of cloth down onto the inhabitants before descending like an angel and proceeding to a decorated pavilion prepared especially for his visit. On other occasions, he arranged torchlit performances of classical dance for visiting foreign dignitaries, on the terraces of Angkor Wat. For diplomatic receptions, he would sometimes compose romantic ballads, which he would sing himself, in a light, almost falsetto tenor, to please the guests. In the 1960's, he made several feature films, starring in them and directing them himself. He edited French-language magazines and a Khmer-language comic monthly. He wrote an immense number of letters, taking issue particularly with books, films, or articles in the foreign press that suggested that Cambodia was small and undeveloped, or that he ruled it as if it were a personal possession. Writings that compared Cambodia to paradise and Sihanouk with the kings of Angkor, on the other hand, earned indulgent praise.

"Cambodia" the Musical

If "Cambodia" can be conceived of in these years as an ongoing musical drama, then Sihanouk was the director, scriptwriter, lead singer, and producer rolled into one. To carry the image further, he also wrote many of the reviews, and even collected money at the door, in the form of hundreds of millions of dollars in aid from foreign powers.

For the great majority of Cambodia's rural poor, the prince's genuine concern for them was a contrast to the off-handed, exploitative style of the French and previous rulers. Gathered at his feet, they enjoyed hearing about Cambodia's greatness, Sihanouk's love life, and the evil intentions of other powers.

Norodom Sihanouk

1922: Born in Phnom Penh to Prince Norodom Suramarit, a king's grandson, and Princess Sisowath Kossomak, daughter of the reigning king.

1941: Chosen by French to succeed his grandfather as king.

1945: Accepts short-lived independence from Japanese occupying army; after five months, French return, reassert control.

1946: With French advice, Sihanouk issues constitution that permits political parties.

1949: Cambodia accepts "50 percent independence" from France.

1952: Sihanouk embarks on one-man Crusade for Independence.

1953: French grant full independence to Cambodia.

1955: Sihanouk abdicates throne in favor of his father; founds political movement, the Sangkum, which then sweeps national elections. Marries Monique Izzi.

1955–1970: Sangkum monopolizes political power in Cambodia.

1960: King Suramarit dies; Sihanouk becomes Cambodian chief of state.

There was no tradition in Cambodia of criticizing a ruler, and no limits were placed on the amount of praise that could be heaped on a particular chief of state. Like many previous rulers, Sihanouk surrounded himself with people who amused him and who could avoid hard work by counting on his gifts. Many foreign journalists, perhaps sincerely convinced that Cambodia was identical to the prince, praised him lavishly, and it seems likely that by the mid-1960's Sihanouk was almost invisible amid all the propaganda.

1963: Sihanouk suspends U.S. aid to Cambodia.

1970: Sihanouk is overthrown, while abroad, by his own government. Almost immediately sets up a government-in-exile in Beijing, allied with Communists, in bid to regain power.

1973: Sihanouk visits Cambodia briefly, meets Communist leaders.

1975: Returns home after Communist victory as figurehead chief of state.

1976: Resigns office, is placed under house arrest in Phnom Penh.

1979: Released to plead cause of Communists at the United Nations after Vietnamese capture of Phnom Penh; goes into exile in China and North Korea.

1982: Sihanouk joins coalition government-in-exile with Communists and former prime minister Son Sann.

1985–1989: Resigns from and rejoins coalition several times. Presides over several fruitless international meetings on "Cambodian problem."

1989: Forces loyal to Sihanouk form "non-Communist resistance" with Son Sann troops. Cambodia engulfed in civil war.

Little by little, however, while Cambodians poured through the school system Sihanouk hastily and generously set up, and as war flared up in neighboring Vietnam, Cambodia's export economy faltered. Economics had never interested Sihanouk, and he had allowed state-owned enterprises to be poorly run. In the meantime, opportunities for employment in the government diminished, and discontent increased. By 1965–1966, Sihanouk's domineering, self-involved manner started to grate on people who felt entitled to their own ideas about their country, or who thought that Sihanouk should share power in governing Cambodia. Some of this opposition came from former members of the political parties smashed by the prince in 1955. Other opponents could be found in the Chinese and Chinese-Cambodian commercial elite and in the ranks of the clandestine Communist Party of Kampuchea (CPK), reconstituted in 1960. By the late 1960's, the CPK began a campaign of armed resistance to the prince, and other opponents became more vocal. In March 1970, when Sihanouk was abroad, the National Assembly voted him out of office as chief of state—a position he had held since the death of King Suramarit ten years before.

At that point, Cambodia plunged into a whirlpool of war and revolution that lasted for many until 1979 and for others well into the 1980's and beyond.

No one predicted these developments, or the possibility of Sihanouk's losing power, when the prince embarked on a program of "Buddhist socialism" in the late 1950's. Knowing what happened later makes it hard to recapture the optimism and naïveté of this prerevolutionary time, but it is important to do so, in fairness to Sihanouk himself and to the genuine contributions he made to Cambodia's modernization.

Sihanouk's Achievements

Cambodia had emerged more or less unscathed from the First Indochina War and the departure of the French. Its steady exports of rice, rubber, and pepper earned enough money overseas to pay for government programs, and the budget was enhanced by foreign aid from a wide range of Communist, neutral, and anti-Communist countries. In 1955, Sihanouk had chosen a neutral position in the cold war that was then raging between the United States and its allies on the one hand and the Soviet Union and its allies (including China) on the other. The Prince

Prince Norodom Sihanouk (1982). Sihanouk ruled Cambodia as King, Prime Minister, and Chief of State between 1941 and 1970. He was a captive of the Communists in Phnom Penh until 1978. Since 1979 he has lived in China and North Korea and has been active in Cambodia's government-in-exile. When this photo was taken, the prince was 59 years old. James G. Gerrand saw no value in Cambodia's four million people taking sides: "When the elephants fight, the grass is trampled," he would say, citing a Cambodian proverb. Moreover, now that French protection was removed, he was suspicious of Thailand and the anti-Communist government that had just been set up in South Vietnam. Both countries were allied to the United States. The Prince felt that taking sides in the cold war would result in his being either swallowed up by these two powers or permanently subordinated to them, serving the United States. Like many Cambodian leaders before and since, he opted for a risky foreign policy that put Cambodian interests first.

His policy meant that he spent the next fifteen years balancing Communist and non-Communist influences. Flattered by praise from the leaders of Communist China—including the prime minister, Zhou En-lai—and annoyed by his cool reception in the United States, where some officials called his neutral policy "immoral," Sihanouk decided to inaugurate some kind of socialism in Cambodia.

Buddhist Socialism

The brand he chose, called "Buddhist socialism" or "Khmer socialism," was in effect a celebration of the status quo with some harmless socialist aspects, such as a lackadaisical manual-labor program for government workers, overlapping economic plans, and many people on the government payroll. There was no redistribution of wealth, no labor movement (strikes were in fact illegal), no farmers' organizations, and no writings, except Sihanouk's own, to explain how Cambodia fitted into a wider socialist tradition.

Sihanouk justified his creation in historical terms. He looked at Angkor and interpreted it in terms of the harmony and cooperation that, he said, had always existed between rulers and ruled. The relations between Jayavarman VII and his people were the same as those between

"Prince Papa" and the twentieth-century Khmer. The king and his people, then and now, saw eye to eye. Society in the 1950's, as in the past, was welded together; everyone had a proper place and a proper role, except for those opposed to Sihanouk's ideas, who were dismissed as "un-Khmer" and, if they were vocal enough, were thrown in prison without trial and occasionally shot.

In the late 1950's, pressures on the Cambodian economy from inside the country and abroad were less severe than they were later. The Vietnam War, which shaped Cambodian history after 1965 or so, had not yet broken out. Political opposition to the prince was disorganized and weak. Sihanouk's popularity at this time as Cambodia's father of independence, working full-time to modernize his country, was at an all-time high.

More importantly, the prince at this stage still listened to advice—from his parents, from French and British advisors, and from senior cabinet members like Son Sann and Penn Nouth, who had no personal ambitions and made sensible suggestions when Sihanouk succumbed, as he often did, to overwork, melancholia, or bad temper.

For the Americans, the Thai, and the South Vietnamese, Sihanouk was an obstacle and a nuisance. He was friendly with Communist China, whose soldiers, only a few years before, had come close to defeating the Americans in Korea. He thought that progress for Cambodia was more important than fighting communism or forming an alliance with America. He also refused to take orders from neighboring states.

American Opposition

For all these reasons, in 1959, the pro-American government in South Vietnam plotted with a Cambodian provincial governor named Dap Chhuon to overthrow the prince. The Vietnamese provided gold ingots, radio equipment, and technical advice to Chhuon, who proposed to lead the province of Siem Reap, containing Angkor, into rebellion against Phnom Penh on the grounds that Sihanouk was "pro-Communist." The American Central Intelligence Agency was aware of the plot but failed to notify Sihanouk, even providing Chhuon with a radio transmitter linked to the American Embassy in Saigon to keep its officers informed.

The plot came apart in February 1959. It is possible that Chhuon tried to back off and informed the prince about the plot, but Sihanouk probably knew enough already from the Chinese and French ambassadors. In any case, troops were sent to Siem Reap, and Chhuon was captured and shot. By the end of the year, U.S. involvement in the plot had come to the surface, which angered Sihanouk and permanently strained U.S.–Cambodian relations.

A second, clumsier plot literally backfired in September 1959, when the South Vietnamese sent Sihanouk a suitcase containing high explosives. The suitcase went off prematurely, killing two officials in the Royal Palace.

In the meantime, the Thai had been plotting with a long-time opponent of Sihanouk, the former prime minister Son Ngoc Thanh, who had lived in exile in Thailand since 1955. By 1960, Thanh had a guerrilla army of some one thousand men training in northeastern Thailand.

Sihanouk was right in thinking that Cambodia was surrounded by unfriendly powers, as it had been in pre-colonial times.

"My Enemy's Enemy Is My Friend"

His reaction, however, was delayed until the end of 1963, when he decided to end the American military and economic aid programs and to nationalize the export-import sector of the economy. These moves, which he had been planning for some time, gained him the approval of the Communist Vietnamese, who by now were engaged in a full-scale war against the American-backed South Vietnamese regime in Saigon.

Following the old motto "My enemy's enemy is my friend," Sihanouk sought to ingratiate himself with the Communists, believing that they would win the war. He hoped by such an alliance to gain time, and for Cambodia to retain its independence.

For several years, Cambodians had unofficially been supplying goods to both sides in Vietnam's civil war. After 1965, Vietnamese Communist soldiers, with Sihanouk's secret approval, began to camp inside Cambodia and to use Cambodian territory to ship military equipment to their forces fighting in southern Vietnam. The Cambodian army was under orders not to interfere, and Cambodian military trucks were sometimes used to ferry equipment to the border.

Sihanouk's friendship with foreign Communists contrasted sharply with his harsh treatment of local ones. In early 1963, fearing arrest by his police, Saloth Sar, Son Sen, and Ieng Sary, high-ranking figures in the secret Communist Party of Kampuchea (CPK), fled Phnom Penh and hid in the forest of eastern Cambodia, where they were protected by Vietnamese Communists. The three men had become acquainted in France in the 1950's, and were to remain important in the CPK for many years.

As the war in Vietnam intensified (U.S. combat troops began arriving in 1965), Sihanouk tried to get foreign powers to guarantee Cambodia's frontiers. Many states agreed to do so, but neither South Vietnam nor Thailand wanted to say that Sihanouk alone could declare where the borders were. Moreover, their leaders, contemptuous of Sihanouk, saw no reason to play his game. The Vietnamese Communists agreed to Sihanouk's terms in order to maintain their alliance with the prince.

In 1958 and 1962, Sihanouk had arranged the elections for the National Assembly, choosing the candidates himself. By and large, he tried to select good candidates, and to balance radicals and conservatives. The candidates were unopposed. In 1966, however, a great many people begged him to appoint them to the Assembly, and so he changed his tactics and let candidates compete against each other openly, within the Sangkum movement.

Sihanouk had always treated the Assembly as a meaningless body, and he expected that the winners in 1966 would be yes-men (and -women), as all members of the Assembly usually had been. But the candidates who were elected owed nothing to his patronage. This is important, for it was the 1966 Assembly that voted Sihanouk out of office four years later.

A New Minister and a Massacre

Sihanouk appointed General Lon Nol, the commander of Cambodia's army, to be prime minister. Lon Nol was nine years older than Sihanouk and had served him faithfully since the early 1950's. He was deeply patriotic, but he seldom expressed his views. Instead, he spent most of his time building up loyalties in the officer corps and hunting down opponents to Sihanouk, whether Communist or pro-American.

In early 1967, a peasant uprising broke out in northwestern Cambodia, where Lon Nol's soldiers had been attempting to commandeer the rice harvest to collect taxes on it. In 1966, tens of thousands of tons of rice had passed secretly across the border to South Vietnam, causing losses of export taxes to the government.

Communist involvement in the uprising has never been proved, but it occurred near the region of Samlaut, favored by Communist forces in the earlier Indochina War. Probably it was a result of local grievances. In any case it was brutally suppressed. Sihanouk later said that he had "read somewhere" that "over 10,000" people, presumed to be rebels, had been killed over the next few months. Obviously Sihanouk had ordered the repression himself. Government casualties were very light.

The rebellion marked a turning point in Sihanouk's years in power. From then on, he seldom hesitated to approve violent measures against opponents, particularly those he suspected of Communist connections. Students in high schools and universities were vulnerable, and in the late 1960's many students "disappeared" from one day to the next. None of them was ever put on trial, and few were ever seen again.

Many Communisms, Many Cambodians

Sihanouk was also distressed by developments in China, where the tumultuous Cultural Revolution, set in motion by Mao Zedong, encouraged students to rebel against authorities and to claim that Mao's thought, enshrined in a short book of quotations, was a Bible for revolutionaries everywhere. Sihanouk's response was to send his foreign minister to Beijing to reassert Cambodia's friendship with China, while at home he cracked down on local Chinese and Cambodian students who wore Mao badges to school or had been heard to praise the Cultural Revolution.

A revolution was the last thing Sihanouk wanted in Cambodia. In 1968 he began edging back toward some kind of relations with the United States. These moves, in turn, undermined the confidence of the Vietnamese Communists in their alliance with him, and by the end of the year Cambodian forces had begun attacking Vietnamese bases inside Cambodia, including some in the remote northeast, where Saloth Sar and other officials of the CPK had been concealed since the end of 1966. The Cambodian Communists, in turn, had become impatient with Vietnamese "guidance," but for the moment there was little they could do about it.

The situation grew worse in 1969. A great deal of Cambodia's rice was still being smuggled into Vietnam, and those who took it there avoided paying Cambodian taxes. In several parts of the country where guerrilla bases had been established, fighting intensified between Communists and Cambodian army units. Sihanouk's army was poorly trained for combat, having been used primarily for parades and public works, but the scope of Communist infiltration of Cambodia, and army casualties, angered many army officers. This anger, building up in the course of 1969 and early 1970, was a major cause of the coup against the prince.

Governing Cambodia single-handedly had grown harder and harder every year. Economic and military problems multiplied, and opposition from radicals and conservatives increased. Sihanouk, however, was unwilling to let go.

The rising discontent was traceable in part to the hundreds of thousands of young men and women who had completed primary school, and some high school, and the tens of thousands who had enrolled in Cambodia's new universities, hoping to improve their economic and social positions. Students were also returning from university training abroad, often with high expectations. Most of these people owed their education to the high priority Sihanouk placed on it as a means of modernizing the country, but they were not grateful to him. There were not enough jobs to absorb them, and they became restless with Sihanouk's one-man rule.

Major Motion Pictures

The prince seems to have known that his popularity was diminishing. One of his reactions was to throw himself headlong into making full-length movies.

Between 1966 and 1969, Sihanouk made nine of these. He wrote the scripts, selected the actors, wrote some of the music, and directed. The movies were expensive to make, but none of the actors were paid. In several, Sihanouk himself appeared as a romantic lead, playing opposite his wife. No one dared to comment on his lack of training or the simplicity of the scripts. As for the prince, he clearly found the movies a relief after trying to run the country. People anxious to please him, including foreign diplomats and correspondents, praised the films extravagantly. Most other observers thought that they were well-meant but amateur. Some of them, dealing with the antics of the idle rich in Phnom Penh, were also offensive to many rural Khmer, whose annual income seldom exceeded the equivalent of $150.

But in the movies, as in everything he did, Sihanouk was unstoppable. By this time, it seems, he thought of Cambodia as a personal possession, and its people as his children. Anything he did, in his view, was beyond criticism, for the benefit of the nation.

To raise revenue for the government, in 1969 Sihanouk inaugurated a gambling casino in Phnom Penh. As far as revenue was concerned it was a huge success, but hundreds of rich and poor Cambodians went bankrupt, many businesses collapsed, and several men and women committed suicide after losing everything at its tables. People blamed Sihanouk and his family for the disasters, and the prince reluctantly agreed to close the casino at the end of 1969.

In 1969 and early 1970, Communist military pressure, student discontent, and anger at Sihanouk's films and the casino combined into an explosive mixture. Sihanouk's high-handed treatment of the National Assembly over the years had also alienated this crucial group.

Two Trips to France

At this time, Lon Nol was in France for medical treatment, and government business fell to the vice-premier, Sihanouk's cousin, Sisowath Sirik Matak, recently Cambodia's ambassador to Japan. Matak, eight years older than Sihanouk, was efficient, aloof, and relatively pro-

Cartoon on a wall, Phnom Penh, 1970, depicting Norodom Sihanouk "crossed out" after being deposed a few months before.   Author

American. He was convinced that Cambodia's economy needed to be freed from state control, and that Vietnamese Communist troops should not be allowed to take shelter in the country.

He was on a collision course with Sihanouk, but he was not frightened by the prince, and stood his ground. He was also on a collision course with the Vietnamese Communists which was to prove fatal to the country.

In January 1970, Sihanouk too left Phnom Penh for medical treatment in France. He was suffering from the effects of diabetes, obesity, and hypertension. While he was gone, Sirik Matak dismantled some state funding bodies, increased the size of the army, and intensified attacks in the press against Vietnamese Communist occupation of Cambodia. When Lon Nol returned from France in February, he found that discontent with Sihanouk was widespread, and that plans for a coup d'état among the army officer corps were well advanced.

Sihanouk lingered in France, hoping for conditions to deteriorate in Cambodia to such an extent that Sirik Matak would beg him to return. Instead, riots in early March against the two Vietnamese Communist embassies in Phnom Penh, set off with Sihanouk's approval, got out of hand, and the embassies were sacked. Mobs also attacked Vietnamese residential areas of Phnom Penh. What Sihanouk had intended as a warning to Hanoi became an outbreak of racist anger by Cambodian mobs. Many in the mobs blamed Sihanouk for favoring the Vietnamese.

Over the next few days Sirik Matak and his supporters put pressure on Lon Nol to support a coup d'état. Lon Nol, whose career owed everything to the prince, was reluctant to join them, but when Sirik Matak threatened to shoot him in a predawn confrontation, he finally agreed.

On March 18, the National Assembly voted 73–3 to remove Sihanouk from office as chief of state, a position he had held since inventing the position in 1960. He had presumed it would be his for life.

An era of one-man rule had ended, ironically, with a vote. The prince heard the news in Moscow, where he was about to board a plane to Beijing, his last stop before returning home. He was stunned. He had counted on Lon Nol's loyalty and his own political skills for too long. Of Lon Nol, he remarked later, "He was my own right hand, and I had no defense against him when he hit me in the face."

Over the next few months, the pace of events accelerated. Lon Nol and Sirik Matak, although popular at first, were unable to halt corruption or train the army fast enough to expel the Vietnamese. As a result, the best army units were cut to pieces in 1970 and 1971 by North Vietnamese forces, now allied with Sihanouk, who had formed a united front consisting primarily of Communists from his exile in Beijing. In a radio broadcast, he addressed the Khmer people as his "brothers and sisters" rather than as his "children," and told them to "go into the jungle and join the guerrillas." Ironically, the "guerrillas" were members of the CPK whom Sihanouk had been trying to destroy only weeks before. CPK recruiters, in rural areas, claimed that they were fighting

Political poster in Phnom Penh, 1971, depicting workers, soldiers, and peasants dethroning Sihanouk the year before. Sihanouk's patrons, the Communist Chinese and Vietnamese, are seen fleeing to the right. James G. Gerrand

Youthful Communist combatants, lined up for a photograph, 1972. These young girls were trained, during the civil war, to bear arms and to perform other military roles for the revolution. Serge Thion

to reinstate "Prince Papa" who had been, only weeks before, their "Enemy Number One."

By the end of 1970, Cambodia became the Khmer Republic, abolishing the monarchy that had served its people, well and badly, for over a thousand years.

Lon Nol and Sirik Matak, however, knew little about democracy, and wartime conditions made it impossible for them to control the country. Over the next two years, they lurched from crisis to crisis. Meanwhile, much of the countryside passed out of their control. Sirik Matak, the abler of the two, was never able to match Lon Nol's power base in the army, and by 1972 he had become a minor figure. Lon Nol suffered a serious stroke in 1971 but was sustained in office by his cronies and by massive military support from the United States. In 1973, he approved the U.S. bombing of the countryside, which inflicted heavy casualties in areas previously undamaged by the war but postponed a Communist military victory for two more years.

Enter the Red Khmer

In 1973, the United States dropped more bombs on Cambodia with which it had never been at war, than it dropped on Japan in 1944–1945. A U.S. Air Force general explained the campaign as being "the only war in town," because U.S. planes had by then been forbidden by the Congress to bomb Vietnam.

Enraged by the bombing, and blaming the "Americans and their puppets" for the civil war, the CPK, or "Red Khmers," as they were called, recruited thousands of young men and women between the ages of twelve and twenty into the Party and into their armed forces. Nearly all the newcomers were from very poor families. Once they joined the Party, they were told in private that Sihanouk was the Party's enemy and that their poverty was traceable to Cambodia's "feudal" past, to "imperialism," and to the "exploiting classes" in Phnom Penh. Many of them believed these explanations. They enjoyed the new respect and responsibility they were given and the weapons they received. They fought hard to liberate their country.

Lon Nol's troops were also brave, but many of their officers were corrupt. They avoided combat, sold weapons and equipment to the enemy, and padded their payrolls with nonexistent soldiers. In one battle in 1971, troops retreating to Phnom Penh complained when they arrived that they had not been paid for several months. Their officers, it turned out, had taken the money for themselves.

After the United States and the Vietnamese Communists signed a ceasefire at the beginning of 1973, which led to the fall of the South Vietnamese government and the reuniting of Vietnam, Vietnamese troops withdrew from Cambodia and left the war in the hands of their Cambodian allies. The war dragged on until 1975. During this time, over a million refugees flooded into Phnom Penh, where they lived in appalling conditions. Lon Nol, half paralyzed, presided over Cambodia as it came apart.

In early 1975, Communist forces succeeded in blockading the Mekong River, thus preventing rice and other supplies from reaching the capital. Their rockets and mortars, in the outer suburbs of the city, shelled the commercial center, killing hundreds of civilians as they tried to lead ordinary lives. Lon Nol was made to resign, given a million dollars, and flown into exile. At the airport, looking back on the last five years of Cambodian history, he burst into tears.

It was too late for compromise, and the CPK had never been interested in negotiations. At the last moment, the Americans tried to enlist Sihanouk on their side, but the prince refused to play, and the U.S. ambassador was flown out of Phnom Penh by helicopter, with the Embassy flag tucked under his arm.

A week later came April 17, 1975. Communist forces—many of them teenagers, heavily armed, silent, and dressed in black cotton pajamas, like most Cambodian peasants—began entering the city.

That morning, a Cambodian working for an American newspaper, trying up to the last minute to do his job, sent a telegram from the post office in Phnom Penh—the last independent telegram to reach the outside world for several years. It read:

I alone in post office. Losing contact with our guys. I have so numerous stories to cover. I feel rather trembling. Do not know how to file stories. How quiet the streets. Every minute changes. With small typewriter I shuttle between post office and home. May be the last cable today and forever.

Revolution in Cambodia

Between April 17, 1975, and the beginning of 1979, the Cambodian people were subjected to the most intense, rapid, and far-reaching social changes in their history. The revolution led by the CPK overturned nearly every Cambodian institution. Towns and cities were emptied; schools, markets, and hospitals were closed; money was abolished; and freedom of movement was halted. Buddhist monks were turned out of their monasteries. Everyone in the country was put to work as peasants or factory workers. In the process at least one person in seven—over a million Cambodians in all—died as a result of revolutionary policies.

Nearly everyone who survived into the 1980's lost close relatives and friends, sucked into the whirlpool of the "Pol Pot time." Some lost

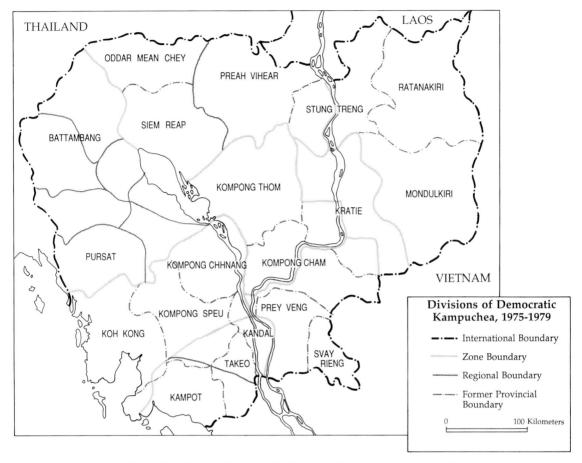

everyone in their family, and many had stood by helplessly watching their relatives dying, or being killed. Memories of these horrific losses have left the survivors permanently scarred, uncertain of themselves, and slow to regain their mental and emotional balance.

What happened in Cambodia in 1975–1979? Who was in charge? Where did their ideas come from? Did they mean to kill a million people? Why did no one intervene? These are questions that survivors often ask themselves when they talk about the "Pol Pot time" or try to explain Cambodia to strangers.

Stages of the Revolution

The revolutionary period breaks into several stages. The first of these, a sort of honeymoon period, lasted from April 1975 to the beginning of 1976, when a constitution was proclaimed, elections were organized, and the CPK emerged, without admitting its name, as the most powerful force in Cambodian life. During these months, those evacuated from the cities were subjected to questioning, propaganda, and humiliation, and were put to work at agricultural tasks, but in comparison with what happened to everybody later, they were treated relatively well. During this time, however, hundreds of men discovered to have been officers in Lon Nol's army or government officials were imprisoned or, in many cases, executed on the spot. People from the cities learned to lie about the past and to respect and obey a mysterious body known only as *angkar padevat* (the revolutionary organization) or *angkar loeu* (the higher organization)—code names for the CPK.

In early 1976, the regime named itself Democratic Kampuchea (D.K.) but still kept the existence of the CPK a secret. Its flag portrayed Angkor Wat, in yellow, on a red background. Until Democratic Kampuchea was proclaimed, the regime had used a plain red flag, without any decorations.

A Super Great Leap Forward

The second phase, when the CPK tested its ability to run the country, lasted until about November 1976. During these months, Pol Pot and his closest colleagues tightened their grip on the central administration. They drafted a secret Four-Year Plan and discussed the document in

Cambodian guerrillas marching in Thailand, early 1979. The uniforms are identical to those worn by the Communist troops under Pol Pot.   James G. Gerrand

Pol Pot

1928: Born as Saloth Sar in Kompong Thom, Cambodia.

1949–1952: Studies electronics in Paris, earns no degree.

1953–1954: Returns to Cambodia; joins Vietnamese-led resistance to French.

1955–1963: While a teacher in a junior high school in Phnom Penh, is active in Cambodia's secret Communist movement.

1956: Marries Khieu Ponnary, also a revolutionary.

1960: Helps to found the Communist Party of Kampuchea (CPK), and is elected to its central committee.

1963: Becomes secretary of CPK central committee, flees to forest to avoid arrest. He remains in the countryside and abroad until 1975.

1965–1966: Visits North Vietnam, China, and North Korea.

1970: Sihanouk overthrown in anti-Communist coup. CPK forms alliance with him and Vietnamese to remove new government from power.

1975: Phnom Penh falls to forces of the "revolutionary organization."

Party circles. The Plan called for the collectivization of Cambodian agriculture, in what was called a "super great leap forward"—a phrase borrowed from Mao's China, without acknowledgment. It proposed to raise Cambodian rice harvests to a national average of about a ton and a half an acre—more than twice as high as prerevolutionary yields. The Plan hoped to expand Cambodia's rice exports to finance the purchase

1976: Democratic Kampuchea (D.K.) proclaimed. Saloth Sar takes the name "Pol Pot" and becomes prime minister.

1976: Following a coup attempt, Pol Pot resigns briefly.

1976–1979: Purges in CPK cause the deaths of over 10,000 Party members.

1977: Existence of CPK revealed just before Pol Pot makes visit to China. Fighting breaks out along the border with Vietnam.

1979: Vietnamese armies invade Cambodia, occupy Phnom Penh, set up satellite Cambodian government. Pol Pot flees to Thailand.

1979–1980: Rebuilds D.K. army with Chinese and Thai assistance.

1981: CPK dissolved, but its leaders remain in command of guerrilla army.

1982: Joins a government-in-exile with Prince Sihanouk and former conservative prime minister, Son Sann.

1982–1989: Directs D.K. troops fighting Vietnamese forces in Cambodia. Remains in political control of D.K. segment of coalition, but is inaccessible to reporters, makes no public statements.

1987: Remarries after his first wife is hospitalized.

of agricultural machinery, pesticides, and fertilizers. The Party's motto was, "With rice we have everything." These purchases, in turn, would enable Cambodia's farmers to increase harvests even more, so as to finance a program of industrialization.

The northwest, which had been the most prosperous agricultural region in the country before 1975, was selected to produce most of the rice. In late 1975 and early 1976, hundreds of thousands of "new people," previously evacuated from Phnom Penh, were herded by truck and train from the center and southwest into Battambang and Pursat to join the work force there.

The Party was optimistic. The radio announced that "2,000 years of history" had ended. Cambodians, working collectively instead of for their families or landlords, were thought of as a mighty force whose victories were as "inevitable" as the Party's victory in 1975 had been.

Unfortunately, the Party paid little attention to regional differences, natural resources, or human beings. Its leaders, dazzled by victory, forgot that the country was exhausted and in disorder after a five-year civil war. Markets had been destroyed, transportation was in chaos, and malnutrition was widespread in several areas. Tools, draft animals, pesticides, and fertilizer were nonexistent, or in short supply. Irrigation works were in poor repair. The unpaid labor force, driven from their homes, were confused, hostile, and often inexperienced at cultivating rice or building irrigation works.

Working conditions throughout the country were harsher than any Cambodians had known before, and there was almost no free time. Those accustomed to farm work adjusted relatively quickly to the new demands but worked much longer hours than they had before the revolution.

Throughout the year, work in the fields, building dams, or digging irrigation canals often started before sunrise and lasted until after sunset, with a break for lunch. Many work sites were miles away from villages. This meant that workers often had only four and five hours' sleep a night. One survivor recalls being so tired, sometimes, that she covered the last few yards to her house by crawling on her hands and knees. Another has written: "From six in the morning until the moon began to rise, they yelled at us to grow more rice. We grew more, but it was always taken away."

Excellent Liars

Once a week, and sometimes more frequently, everyone had to attend political meetings, where they were told what was expected of them and asked to make suggestions and to criticize each other. In some areas, criticism led to disappearances. To avoid trouble, everyone praised the revolution. "We learned to hide our thoughts," a Cambodian has said. "We became excellent liars."

The Party's leaders paid no attention to difficulties encountered in fulfilling the Four-Year Plan. As the Plan began to fail, because the goals were too high, the leaders' reaction was not to blame the document or themselves but to search for "counterrevolutionaries" who were working to betray them.

Microbes to Be Burned Out

The third phase of the revolutionary period began around September 1976 and lasted until early 1977. During this period, the Party attacked "enemies" inside its ranks and launched military attacks against Vietnam. In 1977, communal eating was introduced throughout the country. This meant that everyone on a collective farm had to eat together, in a huge, barnlike dining hall. Food was low in quality and badly prepared. Communal eating was very unpopular, because it broke up family units and eroded family relations. For thousands of years, the family had been the basic unit of Cambodian society. By the middle of 1977, Cambodia was like a vast prison farm.

As harvests fell short of quotas, the CPK leaders began to suspect that members of the Party were plotting against them. These "microbes," as Pol Pot called them, were said to be eating away at the CPK. They needed to be "burned in the fire of revolution."

At about this time, the CPK's long-standing hostility toward the Viet-

Two Revolutionary Songs

These songs, among others, were memorized by a Cambodian factory worker who fled the country in early 1976. They were sung in his village in Battambang during political meetings sponsored by the revolutionary organization (the Communist Party) that governed Cambodia at that time.

The Red Flag

Glittering red blood blankets the earth—blood given up to liberate the people: the blood of workers, peasants, and intellectuals; the blood of young men, Buddhist monks, and girls.
The blood swirls away, and flows upward, gently, into the sky, turning into a red, revolutionary flag.

Red flag! Red flag! flying now! flying now!
Don't spare a single reactionary imperialist; drive them from Kampuchea!
Strive and strike, strive and strike, win victory, win victory!

The Summer Wind

As the summer wind blows, the sun shines on the rice fields, where workers and peasants move together. Some have sickles in their hands, and some carry pots of water on their heads.

Look at the ripe rice, as the wind moves across it in waves. The workers are happy in their hearts, working nights and mornings, with no fear of getting tired.

We are overjoyed to be increasing the output of village and district. Our economy has made great steps forward. We have surpluses now, to put in the granaries, to supply the revolution.

KR guerrilla.   James G. Gerrand

namese Communists also broke to the surface. Some of the "microbes" were accused of working secretly for Vietnam. As previous leaders had done, Pol Pot and his colleagues found the Vietnamese a tempting target. They had resented Vietnamese supervision and guidance of the CPK since the 1950's. Now that they had won their independence, they saw Vietnam no longer as an "elder brother," but as an enemy.

By the end of 1976, Pol Pot believed that the Party was filled with enemies. In a speech in December, he said that "a group of traitors has hidden and buried itself inside our flesh and blood."

In response to these suspicions, the Party's secret interrogation center in Phnom Penh, known by the code name S-21, expanded its operations. Between 1976 and January 1979, over 20,000 Party members and other *khmang* (enemies) were questioned, tortured, and put to death on the grounds of a former high school in the Phnom Penh suburb of Tuol Sleng. The existence of the center was a secret, but people in the CPK soon became aware that many important Party members were dropping out of sight. For the last two years of Democratic Kampuchea, most Cambodians who had believed in the Party became frightened and suspicious of each other. Some began plotting against the government. Others began accusing their colleagues, rightly or wrongly, of such plots.

The Reconquest

The final phase of the "Pol Pot time" began in early 1977, when Cambodia launched military attacks against Vietnam, and lasted until the beginning of 1979, when the regime was overthrown. Some D.K. radio broadcasts claimed that Cambodia intended to "reconquer" southern Vietnam, which had been Cambodian territory until the seventeenth century. The CPK may have hoped that Cambodians inside Vietnam would rise up to support their attacks. They were mistaken, but the attacks continued throughout the year, and many Vietnamese villagers were killed.

In the meantime, relations between Vietnam and China were getting worse. Over the years, Vietnam had tried to be neutral in the conflict of ideas between the Communist superpowers, China and the Soviet Union, but by the mid-1970's its leaders, always suspicious of China, had begun to strengthen their alliance with the Soviets. The Chinese, in turn, were suspicious of having a Soviet ally on their southern border. They intensified their support for Democratic Kampuchea.

Vietnam and Democratic Kampuchea were on a collision course. In July 1977, Vietnam signed a treaty with Laos that seemed, to the leaders of Democratic Kampuchea, to revive the idea of "Indochina," dominated by Vietnam. In September, Pol Pot made a five-hour speech admitting the existence of the CPK and giving credit to the Party for every positive development in Cambodian history. Soon afterward, he made a state visit to China, where he received promises of military help.

In late 1977, Vietnamese forces began attacking Cambodia. A major invasion occurred in December. Pol Pot announced that the Vietnamese withdrawal soon afterwards was a D.K. victory. In fact his troops had performed poorly. In private, he accused Communists in the eastern part of the country, bordering Vietnam, of having "Cambodian bodies and Vietnamese minds" and began to execute them secretly. On the last day of 1977, Democratic Kampuchea broke off diplomatic relations with Vietnam.

The final year of Democratic Kampuchea, 1978, was marked by continuous warfare and purges. Chinese military aid enabled the D.K. forces to confront Vietnam, but Vietnamese troops had more combat experience, better leadership, and more sophisticated equipment. To the very end, Pol Pot and his colleagues remained optimistic. They could not accept the idea that the "mighty victory of April 17, 1975," which had liberated Cambodia from its past, could be dismantled by a foreign power.

In December 1978, the Vietnamese launched their final attack, using over 100,000 troops. They occupied Phnom Penh within a couple of weeks. Pol Pot and the other leaders of the CPK fled to the northwest, and eventually to Thailand, where they remained throughout the 1980's. The D.K. era was at an end.

Regional Variations

Another way of looking at the revolutionary period is in terms of regional variations. The revolution did not move at the same pace everywhere in the country. In some areas, conditions were very harsh; in others, people were treated humanely. In some parts of the country, one's chances of survival were relatively good; in others, fatalities may have run as high as one in three inhabitants. Prerevolutionary institutions such as money, schools, markets, and Buddhist monasteries existed nowhere in Cambodia, but there was considerable variation from one part of the country to another, in the ways that revolutionary policies were applied.

In April 1975, when the CPK took power, it divided Cambodia into seven *phumipheak* (geographic zones)—the northwest, north, northeast, east, southwest, center, and west. These corresponded to military zones during the civil war. They were broken down in turn into *damban* (regions). Poor communication and the power of local CPK figures (or the lack of it) meant that conditions varied from zone to zone and also, inside a given zone, from region to region.

There were also variations over time. Some regions with relatively good conditions got worse after 1977, and others that started poorly improved in 1977–1978.

KR guerrillas in woods, 1979.   B. L. Stevens

Some parts of Cambodia in the east, northeast, and sections of the southwest had been under Communist control since before 1975. Local officials were often local people. Local or "base people" were considered friendly to the revolution. In many areas, they had to attend fewer political meetings than evacuees, enjoyed greater freedom of movement, and were allowed to gather and grow extra food. Because they had always been poor, they were not accused of being "imperialists," "exploiters," or "landlords." More importantly, they lived where they had always lived, or nearby. They knew local conditions and local resources. Unlike most newcomers from the towns, "base people" knew how to survive.

In the eastern zone, many CPK officials were veterans of the First Indochina War in the 1950's. Some of them had absorbed more than twenty years of Communist political training, often from the Vietnamese. Others had returned to Cambodia after years of residence in Vietnam. Because most of them were honest and fair and lived among the people, they were widely respected. By 1977 or so, this respect, as well as their past histories, attracted the hostility of the regime.

Similar conditions applied in the northeast, which had been a Communist stronghold since the 1960's. In general, Communists in areas where Vietnamese influence had been strong tended to be more responsive to the needs of local people.

In the northwest, on the other hand, conditions were generally poor. By the beginning of 1976, nearly a million "new people" had been relocated there. About 300,000 of them had been driven out of Battambang City and the surrounding countryside in April 1975. Perhaps as many had been brought into the area from Phnom Penh. The tasks of organizing these newcomers—arranging housing, food, clothing, and tools for them and putting them to work—were enormous, and often beyond the capacities of local leaders.

Wearing Glasses and Other Crimes

The northwest had traditionally been Cambodia's richest rice-producing region, and contained some of the country's most fertile soil. Nonetheless, in the D.K. period, the treatment of people throughout the region was very harsh.

There are several reasons for this. Local party officials, known as "cadre," were poorly trained and had almost no experience of administration. In many areas, they were outnumbered by "new people," who, for their part, had no understanding of revolutionary goals and little patience with their new "masters," often illiterate teenagers. Conflicts were inevitable. Many "new people" were shot for arguing with cadre, or as they tried to escape to nearby Thailand. Others were executed because their previous work as soldiers, teachers, merchants, or bureaucrats made them *khmang* (enemies). In some areas, people with glasses were labeled as "capitalists," and were badly treated. So were people who used foreign words in conversation or complained about conditions.

Executions were never public or explained. Instead, people would be taken from their houses at night or would be invited to "study" or to "gather fruit" while they were working. People taken off in this fashion seldom reappeared. "The worst time of day," a refugee from the northwest has said, "was at sunset, because that was when people would be taken away. Every night we were frightened. The best time was when we woke up, at sunrise, because we knew we had survived another night." Many of the executions were carried out by young soldiers between the ages of twelve and fifteen.

These young people, and those who commanded them, never regretted the deaths of "counterrevolutionaries," as the offenders came to be called. Instead, they sometimes welcomed these deaths. Many survivors recall cadre telling them that "keeping you is not profitable for us; discarding you is no loss." This ominous motto was used throughout the country.

Another reason for harsh conditions in the northwest was that the CPK's leaders wanted the region to produce the largest surpluses of rice in the country. This meant that local Communists were often pressed to deliver unrealistic amounts. One way of reaching the quota was to cut back on the rice set aside to feed the population and to pass it along as "surplus." Many survivors remember that by 1977 they no longer ate rice but were given watery *bawbaw* (rice soup) instead. They were not allowed to look for extra food, and they had to work as hard as ever.

As they grew thinner, they watched the "surpluses" being taken away in trucks. Thousands of them died of malnutrition and overwork.

The national plan also called for new areas to be brought under cultivation in order to increase the harvests. Many of these areas had been avoided by farmers in the past because they were malarial, or lacked water, or both. New people sent into these regions—*dambans* 2, 5, and 6—died by the thousands.

Over time, conditions in the northwest became more stable. Executions were less frequent, food in some areas improved, and experienced cadre were brought in from the southwest to supervise the workers. In parts of the east, on the other hand, conditions grew worse after the war with Vietnam began in 1977. In 1978, tens of thousands of people were herded out of the eastern zone to be resettled elsewhere, but in the process, those in charge sometimes panicked and executed large numbers of the evacuees. By then, purges were burning through the ranks of the CPK.

Prisoners of the City

Between 1975 and 1979, perhaps 40,000 people worked in Phnom Penh. Most of them were employed by government ministries or factories. Food was more plentiful than in the northwest, but city dwellers under Democratic Kampuchea were kept prisoner where they worked. They were not allowed to walk around the city, and could visit their husbands or wives (who often worked elsewhere) only once or twice a month. There were no diversions; even kicking a soccer ball around was forbidden by the authorities. Now and then, workers would be assembled to listen to speeches by high Party officials, who arrived wearing peasant costume, as everyone did, but who were driven in enormous cars. One survivor recalled the foreign minister, Ieng Sary, who drove in a Mercedes Benz, as "very fat. He must have had much more to eat than any of us."

Most survivors of Democratic Kampuchea recall the differences in privilege that swiftly developed between members of the Party and the revolutionary army on the one hand and the rest of the country on the other. The most noticeable were that Party members and soldiers ate much more food and worked shorter hours. They were also the only Cambodians allowed to wear watches, carry pens and weapons, and listen to portable radios. For many illiterate peasants, these privileges were greater than any they had ever enjoyed. In gratitude they obeyed "the organization," which became, as one of them later remembered, "like a mother and a father to me." They also enjoyed power, and using their weapons against "enemies of the revolution."

Revolutionary Ideas

What ideas lay behind the Cambodian revolution? Why were tens of thousands of Cambodians drawn into the ranks of the CPK? Revolutionary ideas played a large part in their conversion. A refugee who left Cambodia in 1976 has said, "At first the ideas seemed good." Many thousands agreed with him, and were disillusioned later.

Probably the most important new idea was that society was made up of conflicting classes. Prerevolutionary Cambodians had been aware of rich and poor, masters and servants, and so on, but they had taken these conditions as unchangeable, and thus to be endured. The CPK saw class relationships in terms of unending conflict. For a just, equal society, the revolutionaries argued, workers and peasants had to overthrow the "ruling classes" and take command of the country in their place. Those they would replace included not only the rich and powerful, but all authority figures—teachers, monks, parents, and grandparents—who stood in the path of the revolution. In the process society would revolve, or overturn like a wheel.

The revolution was to be led by a small group of revolutionaries—the CPK—itself led by an even smaller group to whom other members had to swear absolute obedience. The leaders of the CPK, without being chosen in an election by workers and peasants, were supposedly totally dedicated to the formation of a just, equal society, which they would lead, as spokespeople for those Cambodians who had formerly, in Pol Pot's words, "lived in disgrace and the darkest shadows, without any light." Under the leadership of the Party, these conditions supposedly would be transformed.

Cambodia had often had absolute rulers, but these men had never suggested that the relationships inside society should change, demanding respect because they were in charge of the country rather than because they wanted to overturn it.

Part of the excitement that many people felt about revolutionary ideas was that they had never been tried in Cambodia before. This excitement had drawn Pol Pot and his friends toward communism in the 1950's. Twenty-five years later, the Party made new promises to people who had always been powerless. The revolution and the Party seemed to offer them new measures of respect, responsibility, and power.

Everything in life was seen in terms of class warfare and the struggle among classes for justice and power. It was considered inevitable that workers and peasants would be victorious over "counterrevolutionary" people, but even in victory everyone was told to be on the lookout for "enemies." As in China and the Soviet Union, politics could command other aspects of life. Revolution was most appealing to young men and women because they were now free to move in any direction and also to the poorest Cambodians, who stood to benefit from it.

Winners and Losers of Class War

The victims of the revolution were far more numerous than the beneficiaries. Cambodian rice farmers and their families made up four fifths of the country's population. They were supposedly the "winners" in the revolution. They had been used to harsh conditions and hard work for centuries, and to exploitation by the rich. Supposedly, the revolution was being fought on their behalf.

Nonetheless, to many of them the revolution made little sense. They couldn't understand why they were not allowed to eat together; why they couldn't travel from village to village when they felt like it, or hunt and fish; why there was no money; or why their children were taken off to work in other zones. Many regretted the disappearance of Buddhism, and the festivals that had punctuated the year. They resented their discomfort, and having no free time. Most of them saw no privileges or comfort coming to them from the revolution. Instead, they worked harder than ever before, ate less, and watched each other sicken with malaria and malnutrition. Out of the corners of their eyes, they sometimes saw young cadre and soldiers feasting in the shade.

The leaders of the organization paid little attention to these perceptions or to conditions in the countryside. They were convinced that they were right. They were sure they knew what the farmers wanted; they also knew that they were running out of time. For these reasons, they imposed their will on everyone, without asking for anyone's opinion. They also imposed economic change at a breakneck pace. They may have been afraid that if they took the revolution a step at a time, it would never succeed.

Within this framework, another important idea was that Cambodia had to be totally independent, owing allegiance to no outside powers. It had to wage its revolution, "building and defending the country"

entirely with its own resources. As Pol Pot later said, "We fought our revolution with empty hands." The idea of independence made many Cambodians proud, but it soon led to conflict with Vietnam and kept the regime from accepting foreign aid that might have saved tens of thousands of lives in 1975–1976.

A Balance Sheet

Despite the attractiveness of some of these revolutionary ideas, it is impossible to draw up a "balance sheet" of the D.K. period without placing a million dead Cambodians, who died as victims of the revolution, on one side of the equation. There is no evidence that the leaders of Democratic Kampuchea intended so many people to be lost. Instead, they believed so fervently in the revolution that they probably believed it would succeed at a far lower human cost.

Whether the deaths were intentional or not, however, there is no evidence that the leaders ever regretted them. When pressed, leaders of the Party referred in the 1980's to five thousand deaths in the D.K. period, blaming three million on the Vietnamese. In 1988, one D.K. official even suggested that the missing Cambodians were "hiding in the forest," fearful of the Vietnamese.

All that these men and women regretted was that the revolution had failed. They blamed the failure on "enemies" rather than on revolutionary ideas or on themselves. Indeed, ten years after being overthrown, the same leaders hoped to regain power, to demonstrate that the revolution and their leadership had been correct all along.

Cambodia's killing fields. Skulls from a Communist burial ground, arranged in rows (1981). There are hundreds of these burial grounds in Cambodia. Perhaps a million people died of overwork, malnutrition, and executions under Pol Pot. Kelvin Rowley

Genocide and Cambodia

The word "genocide" means literally "the killing of a race, or people." It is most frequently used to describe the killing of European Jews by Nazi Germany before and during World War II. In 1948, the United Nations passed a resolution that condemned the *"intentional destruction of a national, ethnic, racial or religious group by means such as killing, serious bodily or mental harm, the conditions of life to which a group is subjected, the prevention of births within a group, or forcibly transferring children of one group to another group."*

Were the million people who died in Cambodia between 1975 and 1978 victims of a genocidal policy? If they were, Pol Pot and other leaders of Democratic Kampuchea can be brought to trial at the International Court in The Hague, Netherlands. Throughout the 1980's, there were many attempts to charge Pol Pot with genocide. These ran into two major problems. One was that so many members of the United Nations supported Pol Pot because of his opposition to Vietnam. These included China, the United States, and most of their allies. The second difficulty was that the U.N. resolution said

They never paused to think why so few people accepted ideas that were so violent, so untested, and so enormously risky. They were convinced that they were right and that ordinary men and women would follow them toward an ideal society.

In rejecting their leadership, their methods, and their ideas, the nothing about a country eliminating its *political* and *economic* enemies, as dictatorships have always done. Millions of political enemies died in China in the civil war of the 1920's, in the Soviet Union in the 1920's and 1930's, and in Communist China in the 1950's and 1960's—to say nothing of the deaths in smaller countries.

Cambodian Buddhist monks, Moslem Chams, and ethnic Chinese were deliberately persecuted by Democratic Kampuchea. Tens of thousands of them died from hardship or executions.

Were these deaths "genocide" in the terms of the U.N. resolution? Or were they part of a program to "scatter and smash" the political and economic enemies of the regime? If they were, the genocide convention may not apply. This doesn't mean that Pol Pot and his colleagues are innocent. It means that causing the deaths of one Cambodian in seven was not meant, as Hitler's policies were, to eliminate a "national, ethnic, racial, or religious group."

What do you think?

Cambodian people were not stepping backward into the past. Instead, most of them were taking care of their own lives, as they had been led up to then, and were protecting their children's future. They observed the revolution, rejected it, and survived.

Cambodia Since 1979

Cambodia Struggles to Its Feet

In December 1978, a large Vietnamese army, accompanied by much less numerous Cambodian forces, swept into Cambodia. Within two weeks they overthrew the D.K. regime. Pol Pot and his immediate colleagues fled Phnom Penh in helicopters for Thailand. Others marched their troops, and any civilians they could gather together, toward guerrilla bases in the northwest.

For public relations purposes, the Vietnamese denied for several months that their troops had been involved in the campaign against Democratic Kampuchea, claiming that the forces that had seized power were ethnically Khmer representatives of a "Liberation Front," formed at a meeting on the Cambodian–Vietnamese border in December 1978.

Over the next few weeks, the Vietnamese authorities swiftly established a government friendly to them, based on this liberation front, in Phnom Penh. A Kampuchean People's Revolutionary Council was set up three days after Phnom Penh had been taken, and the country was renamed the People's Republic of Kampuchea (P.R.K.) a few days after that. Its President, Heng Samrin, had been a D.K. military commander in the eastern zone until early 1978. The new foreign minister, Hun Sen, then under thirty, had defected from the eastern zone in 1977. Both men remained high-ranking figures in the People's Republic of Kampuchea throughout the 1980's.

Those in command of the new government consisted largely of Cambodians who had defected from Democratic Kampuchea after 1976 or had spent many years—in some cases, most of their grown lives—in Vietnam. There were also some representations of tribal minorities.

The immediate reaction of most other Cambodians to the collapse of Democratic Kampuchea was one of stunned relief. In some villages, news of the invasion encouraged villagers to massacre D.K. cadre. In others, where the cadre had vanished overnight, news of the defeat prompted thousands to think of escaping into Thailand and others to walk across the country to regain their villages and to look for relatives who had disappeared.

Unfortunately, as hundreds of thousands of Cambodians crisscrossed the country trying to put their lives together, the 1978–1979 rice harvest, which was being brought in as the Vietnamese invaded, was largely abandoned in the fields. This meant that very little grain was stored for consumption later in the year, and not enough rice seed was available for planting. Many survivors suffered from malnutrition in 1979 and 1980, and thousands of them, particularly elderly people and children, starved to death. Others were saved by emergency foreign aid, administered largely through the United Nations.

The Vietnamese miscalculated the effect of their invasion on world opinion. What they saw as a liberation as far as Cambodia was concerned, and as a necessary step to protect themselves, was seen in most Western countries and in China as unprovoked aggression. Ironically, Vietnam's reasons for attacking Cambodia—to protect its western frontier from hostile forces—were the same as those that had led the United States to invade Cambodia in 1970.

China's response to the Vietnamese invasion of Cambodia was to invade northern Vietnam in February 1979, using 250,000 troops "to teach Vietnam a lesson" as one of its leaders said. The Chinese withdrew their troops after three weeks, after suffering heavy losses

Phnom Penh market: selling rice, February 1980. Markets and money, abolished by Pol Pot, were brought back into use in 1979–1980.   Grant Evans

Orphans in Battambang, 1980. Hundreds of thousands of young Cambodians lost their parents in the warfare and upheavals of the 1970's. Under the post-1979 government, orphans were given special privileges, as a way of making up for their losses. Grant Evans

and destroying most towns within twenty miles of the frontier. The invasion failed to force Vietnam out of Cambodia.

Before their invasion, the Chinese had promised military aid to the exiled leaders of Democratic Kampuchea. By the middle of 1979, the Thai government agreed to shelter and feed those D.K. forces that had already crossed into Thailand. The U.S. government, then in a pro-Chinese, anti-Vietnamese stage of its foreign policy, made no objection. For Cambodia, the stage was set for a prolonged period of foreign occupation and civil war.

Throughout the 1980's, the Vietnamese maintained tens of thousands of its troops in Cambodia. Militarily, the rulers of Vietnam wanted to keep Democratic Kampuchea from returning to power. Politically, they may have intended to turn Cambodia into part of an Indochinese federation, consisting of Vietnam, Cambodia, and Laos, although they never said so publicly.

For several years, they gave no indication that they would withdraw their troops or reduce their political role. They did little to train a local Cambodian force, and treated opponents of their occupation harshly. Most of all, they kept a sharp eye on the People's Republic of Kampuchea's economy and on its conduct of foreign affairs, making sure that its policies were properly socialist and posed no threat to Vietnam. On a day-to-day basis, however, Vietnamese soldiers behaved politely to Cambodians. Most Vietnamese advisors kept out of sight, and the policies they set in motion were relatively lenient, compared to those of Democratic Kampuchea.

As time went on, the Vietnamese presence aroused resentment among the Khmer. So did the persistence, under the People's Republic of Kampuchea, of Communist ideas. There were human-rights abuses, also, of the sort that had plagued the regimes of Sihanouk and Lon Nol. These included the imprisonment without trial of people thought to be opposed to the People's Republic of Kampuchea, torture and execution, and forced drafts of workers to clear forests and roads for Vietnamese forces in the combat areas of the northwest. Cambodians working for the government were also required to attend long hours of political indoctrination. Many of those invited for further training in Vietnam misinterpreted the invitation as a threat and bolted for the Thai border.

The Vietnamese Settle In

In the 1980's, hundreds of thousands of Vietnamese civilians settled in Cambodia. Accurate statistics about them were hard to obtain, because the People's Republic of Kampuchea played down the numbers, and those opposed to the Vietnamese occupation exaggerated them. A 1986 estimate put the number at roughly 250,000, or less than 5 percent of the population. Many of the newcomers had lived in Cambodia before 1970, and they resumed their former activities, such as shopkeeping in Phnom Penh and commercial fishing in the Tonle Sap. Others were drawn into Cambodia because conditions were easier there than in neighboring Vietnam. This immigration made many Cambodians nervous, and Cambodians overseas who opposed the PRK claimed that the immigrants were part of a conscious Vietnamese policy to overpower the Khmer.

Fears like these, and the People's Republic of Kampuchea's occasionally harsh administration, led tens of thousands of Cambodians to leave Cambodia. They sought refuge first in recently established refugee

People waiting for rice to be distributed, Kompong Thom, 1980. The soldier in the center is Vietnamese.   Grant Evans

camps along the Thai border and later overseas. By the mid-1980's, nearly half a million Cambodians, many of them relatively well educated, had resettled in France, the United States, Canada, Australia, and other countries in the West. The People's Republic of Kampuchea could not afford to lose so many skilled men and women. Another 325,000 Cambodians lived precariously in camps in Thailand, fed and housed by the United Nations and unable to go home or to find refuge in other countries. These refugees formed the recruiting base for resistance forces seeking to drive out the Vietnamese.

Little by little, however, beginning in 1983—partly as a result of foreign pressure, and also because fighting against the Red Khmers and other resistance forces tapered off—the Vietnamese withdrew their troops, and Vietnamese political influence on Cambodia diminished.

New Socialism

After 1981, the People's Republic of Kampuchea openly claimed to be a socialist government, but it disowned the activities of Cambodian Communists between 1960, when Pol Pot was elected to the CPK Central Committee, and the Vietnamese invasion of 1979. The People's Republic of Kampuchea denied that Pol Pot had been a Communist at all. They compared him to Hitler and blamed all the evils of Democratic Kampuchea on him and his colleagues Ieng Sary and Khieu Samphan. The interrogation center at Tuol Sleng was turned into a Genocide Museum, and its displays were modeled on those in Nazi concentration-camp museums in Eastern Europe.

In August, 1979, the People's Republic of Kampuchea conducted a show trial of Pol Pot and Ieng Sary, who were condemned to death, though they were not present to defend themselves. No other D.K. officials were accused of any crimes, and no attempt was made by the

A Refugee's Drawing (1986)

This drawing was made by a sixteen-year-old Cambodian boy, Ra Bony, in 1982, when he was in a refugee camp in Thailand and fighting as a soldier for the non-Communist resistance. Bony told a Western visitor to the camp, who admired the drawing, "These are two ancient mountain warriors of Angkor Wat. I remember seeing them in a book while I was in school before the Pol Pot regime. The teacher said that at one time they had been inside a single body, but because one was good and the other was evil, they broke apart and have been fighting ever since. See, they are tied at the wrists and cannot escape. I think Cambodia is still like this. . . ."

People's Republic of Kampuchea later on to weed out people who had worked for Democratic Kampuchea before 1979 but were now willing to work for the new regime.

Even so, it was impossible for the Vietnamese and their Cambodian colleagues to impose far-reaching socialist ideas, even if they had wanted to do so. Land and factories remained theoretically the property of the state, but it soon became clear that the only policies that would succeed were those that had no connection to those of the Pol Pot era, or that overturned them.

The main concerns of the People's Republic of Kampuchea in 1979–1980 were to survive, to buy time, and to gain popular support. Schools were reopened, money put back into circulation, and Buddhist monasteries allowed to function. The People's Republic of Kampuchea continually attacked "Pol Pot time"—the name they used for the D.K. era—and for several years did little to restrict people's freedom of movement. Many Cambodians took advantage of this freedom to flee the country. Others used it to find their families and reoccupy their homes. Still others, beginning in early 1980, began to travel to and from the Thai border, where a lively trade developed. Cambodians traded gold jewelry (their pre-D.K. "savings accounts") and local products, including sapphires, for consumer goods that were sold, for higher prices, in Phnom Penh. To retain its popularity, the government delayed imposing income or property taxes, which would have been difficult to collect.

By 1980, some Western agencies, as well as Soviet-bloc governments and India, had begun to administer a modest program of humanitarian aid. Military assistance to the regime came from Vietnam and the Soviet Union. Private foreign investment was held back by the fact that the United Nations officially recognized Democratic Kampuchea and by the People's Republic of Kampuchea's reluctance to allow local capitalists, private ownership of property, and private banks to reemerge.

Little by little, the understaffed P.R.K. government gained skills and

A Soviet teacher in a Cambodian university classroom. This class in agricultural econom-ics is being taught in Russian. The U.S.S.R. provided valuable economic aid to Cambodia in the 1980's, when many nations refused to recognize the Vietnamese-sponsored re-gime. Kelvin Rowley

confidence. However, revenues were low, luxuries were rare, and basic services, such as running water and electricity, were in short supply. Throughout the country, problems of health, sanitation, malnutrition, and distrust still hampered the regime, and so did shortages of trained personnel.

Nonetheless, the People's Republic of Kampuchea made heroic ef-forts to overcome difficulties, particularly in the field of education, where they were faced with five years of no schools at all and a decade of neglect. By the late 1980's, over 30,000 teachers were teaching over 1.6 million Cambodian children and young people at various levels. The government was also active in trying to reduce illiteracy among the men and women who had missed out on schooling in the 1970's.

Rebuilding a Nation

In the countryside, Cambodian farmers began growing their own food again and rebuilding the family-based life-style that had characterized Cambodia before 1975. To be sure, new perils, such as land mines, raids by resistance forces, and the disappearance of many market towns made life in the 1980's more dangerous and unhealthy than it had been twenty years before. On balance, however, against tremendous odds, Cambodia began struggling to its feet.

The grandiose collective farms established under Democratic Kampuchea collapsed in 1979, as soon as the cadre fled. So did many of the ambitious irrigation works constructed in 1975–1978, although some

Children help their mother in the fields, Kompong Speu, 1988. The harvest has already taken place. The children are gathering rice straw to use as food for domestic animals. Christine Drummond

sturdily built ones remained in use. Farmers resumed their habit of cultivating rice according to the lay of the land, soil fertility, and drainage, rather than following a geometric "plan."

But it was too early to resume family farming of the kind that had predominated in Cambodia before 1975. So many farmers had been killed or disappeared that villagers throughout the People's Republic of Kampuchea agreed to be banded together into *krom samakki* (solidarity groups) to grow and harvest their crops. These groups, established in 1979 by the government, consisted of between 12 and 15 families, or roughly 70 people, who cultivated between 30 and 50 acres of cropland in common and reported on their activities to representatives of the governing party. Through these groups, the government kept track of everyone in the country, in theory at least. Each family was also allowed to cultivate a small private plot, and was free to trade what it grew privately for other products.

In 1981, the People's Republic of Kampuchea claimed that over 70 percent of Cambodia's agricultural work force was organized into solidarity groups. Eight years later, as economic conditions improved and Vietnamese influence on government policies waned, the percentage dropped sharply, reflecting a tendency for families to cultivate their smaller holdings on their own, calling on help only for planting and harvesting, as they had done in prerevolutionary times. By the end of the 1980's, collectivized farming, introduced under Pol Pot and modified by the People's Republic of Kampuchea, no longer existed in Cambodia.

By the late 1980's, as many of the scars from the D.K. period healed and Cambodia's economy righted itself, there was a noticeable rise in exports and a slight increase in agricultural yields. By 1985, ricelands had risen to half the acreage of prerevolutionary times, or double the figures for 1979. These increases were encouraging, but hardly kept up

Market at Sisophon, northwestern Cambodia, 1981. The currency being used is gold leaf. The women at the market wear Western-style blouses and traditional kramar *(Cambodian turbans).*   Grant Evans

with Cambodia's growing population, and as late as 1989 the government was importing several hundred thousand tons of rice to feed its people.

Informal foreign trade, and smuggling made many Cambodians prosperous, but the government gained little money from these activities, and imports, particularly from the Soviet bloc, outran formal exports by ratios of ten to one.

In mid-1989, the People's Republic of Kampuchea made several changes to its constitution. These were intended to attract foreign support and to increase the government's popularity. One was to declare Buddhism the country's national religion, as it had been in prerevolutionary times, and to allow young men to become monks, instead of restricting the monkhood to men over fifty, as had been the practice since 1979.

Another was to allow private ownership of land and real estate. A third was to change the name of the country and its flag. The new name, introduced in 1989, was the State of Cambodia (S.O.C.). The new flag combined elements of the P.R.K. flag with flags from before 1975.

The death penalty was also abolished at this time to demonstrate an increasing concern for human rights. The rest of the constitution, which vested state power in bodies dominated by the People's Revolutionary Party, was unchanged, but ideology played an increasingly minor role in government decisions, particularly after the spectacular collapse of many Communist regimes in Eastern Europe in 1989 and 1990.

Hun Sen

The government's willingness to experiment with change was connected by many observers to the People's Republic of Kampuchea's dynamic young prime minister, Hun Sen, who was named to the post in 1985. Although technically Number 3 in the P.R.K. administration, he soon became its most visible and articulate spokesman in Cambodia and overseas.

Hun Sen was born into a prosperous peasant family in Kompong Cham in 1952. He joined the Communist resistance against Sihanouk before finishing high school. He was wounded several times, and lost his left eye in the closing stages of the civil war. In 1977, he was a military commander in the eastern zone and fled to Vietnam, apparently

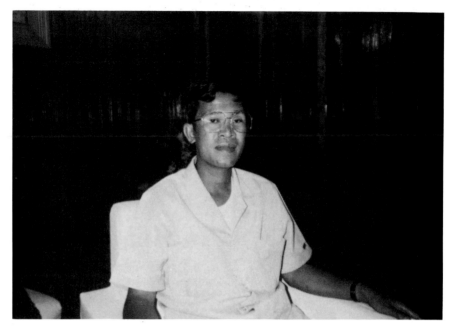

Hun Sen, prime minister of the State of Cambodia.   Nayan Chanda

because he opposed Pol Pot's policies. He returned home with the Vietnamese army in January 1979 and rose rapidly in the ranks of the People's Republic of Kampuchea. Reporters and diplomats who met him in Cambodia and overseas in the late 1980's were impressed by his flexibility, his patriotism, his willingness to take advice, and his genuine political skills.

While many visitors in the late 1980's found grounds for optimism in Hun Sen, in the bustling streets and markets of Phnom Penh, and among the resilient Cambodians themselves, conditions in the country-side were harder to observe and were probably much harsher than they had been before the revolution.

Cambodia faced many problems as it entered the 1990's. Some stemmed from poverty and the country's isolation from development aid from Western countries. One of the largest problems, however, was the continuing civil war.

Resistance to the People's Republic of Kampuchea

Because of support from China, the Association of Southeast Asian Nations (ASEAN), and the United States, Democratic Kampuchea continued to be recognized by the United Nations throughout the 1980's. It was the only government-in-exile to receive such recognition. Its

Tame elephants, Kompong Thom, 1980. Their legs are chained together to prevent escape. Notice the large bells around their necks.   Grant Evans

military forces were sheltered by the Thai and supplied with weapons, ammunition, equipment, and training by the Chinese.

By 1981, however, the horrors of Democratic Kampuchea had been made known to the outside world by refugee accounts, foreign journalists, and the show trial of Pol Pot and Ieng Sary. It was time for the nations backing Democratic Kampuchea to provide it with a more human face, and for someone besides Pol Pot to represent Cambodia at the United Nations.

In this context, someone was needed who might stand in front of the leaders of Democratic Kampuchea, concealing them from view, without removing D.K. military forces from the scene.

Those chosen for the job were Prince Sihanouk, who had been living in exile in Beijing since 1979, and one of his former ministers, Son Sann, who had been trying to form an anti-Communist resistance to the Vietnamese occupation among refugees along the Thai border since 1979. The two men were persuaded to form a coalition with Democratic Kampuchea. This "government"—which controlled no territory, collected no taxes, and depended entirely on foreign powers—was soon recognized by the United Nations. Democratic Kampuchea was the winner in the arrangements, because it retained control over the coalition government's foreign affairs, and thus over its delegation to the United Nations.

The coalition was never united. Its leaders distrusted each other. The troops under their command were unwilling to work together. Occasionally they fought each other instead of the Vietnamese. The coalition was further weakened when high-ranking figures working with Son Sann and Sihanouk plotted among themselves or used funds raised among refugees or from foreign governments for their factions to enrich themselves. Sihanouk himself, as temperamental as ever, resigned from the coalition several times, and spent much of his time writing his memoirs, directing movies, and attacking Son Sann, Hun Sen, and Pol Pot. Nonetheless, as Cambodia's "father," he insisted on playing a major role in any international negotiations. His armed forces, and Son Sann's, though, were smaller, more poorly equipped, and less effective militarily than those of Democratic Kampuchea.

In terms of liberated territory, the resistance accomplished little. By early 1990, however, resistance forces claimed to control several hundred square miles of territory in Cambodia's northwest. The Vietnamese admitted that they had sustained over 50,000 casualties fighting in Cambodia between 1977 and 1989. Most of these had occurred in the 1977–1979 war, but thousands had died later, from land mines, malaria, and ambushes. Casualties among P.R.K./S.O.C. forces and civilians were also high.

After the Vietnamese forces withdrew, renewed fighting broke out between the coalition and the State of Cambodia. The dry season between November and March favored the S.O.C. forces, whose heavy vehicles could move freely on dry ground, while the rainy months between April and October favored the hit-and-run guerrilla tactics of the resistance.

D.K. forces gained food, recruits, and information by terrorizing local people and blaming Vietnam. Sometimes, D.K. troops reminded Cambodians of the grim period of their rule. In some areas, they recited a poem that went:

> *When you eat from a small pot* [in a family]
> *Remember the big pot* [of communal eating].
> *When you wear flowery silks*
> *Don't forget that everyone used to be dressed alike, in black.*
> *When the Vietnamese are gone*
> *Every well will hold a hundred bodies.*

Visitors to Cambodia in 1989–1990 reported that everyone was fearful of a return to power by Pol Pot and hoped for an international settlement that would avert a civil war.

With brief intervals, however, civil war had been devastating Cambodia for twenty years. None of the resistance leaders were interested in compromise with Vietnam or with the State of Cambodia. Instead, they offered Cambodians past political alternatives—monarchy, middle-class democracy, and Communism—that had failed. The State of Cambodia, for all its shortcomings, seemed to many to be willing to make some accommodation with reality and to open itself up to genuine change. After years of political indoctrination, it seemed, most Cambodians were tired of politics, and didn't care what political structure was arranged so long as Pol Pot did not return to power. In the meantime, casualties mounted, and a secure future without bloodshed for Cambodia, or even a breathing spell that gave its people an opportunity to rebuild, remained impossible to predict.

Cambodia Today

There are over seven million ways of writing about Cambodia today. Each Cambodian's experiences are authentic, and slightly different from the those of anyone else. One problem for a writer is to discover common themes among the voices.

Another is that so much of the country is inaccessible to outsiders, because of the civil war or because overland communication is so poor. It is almost impossible to generalize about rural life, even though over 80 percent of Cambodia's people live in the countryside.

A third problem is that "Cambodia" in 1990 includes not only the country itself, but the 320,000 Cambodians along the Thai border and 250,000 more who have resettled overseas. A widow in Phnom Penh, for example, would describe "Cambodia today" differently from a farmer in western Kompong Speu, a trader in the "Site 8" refugee camp in Thailand (one of many) or a teenager in Long Beach, California, where almost 40,000 Cambodians have settled since 1980.

Keeping these difficulties in mind, some important themes emerge from Cambodia's recent history, and affect the ways that Cambodians face the future.

The Fear of Pol Pot

One is the fear that Pol Pot will reemerge and reenact the horrors of 1975–1979. Memories of uncontrolled violence and total domination have driven many Cambodians into mental illness, and all survivors are fearful of Democratic Kampuchea. "War is a horrifying prospect for Cambodians," one of them said in September 1989. "I don't think they could survive another one, physically or mentally." Three years earlier, a Western psychiatrist reported, after several months among Cambodian refugees, that more than half of those he worked with suffered from sleeplessness, nightmares, poor appetites, and estrangement from other people. Similar symptoms have been reported from Cambodians inside the country and overseas.

The People's Republic of Kampuchea and the State of Cambodia tried to channel this fear and resentment into an annual "Day of Hatred," celebrated in May, in which the crimes of Pol Pot were recalled, in ceremonies conducted at village cemeteries, Tuol Sleng, and other sites of violence under Democratic Kampuchea.

Poverty

A second theme is that nearly all Cambodians are still extremely poor. Only a few thousand of them inside the country have access to electricity and running water. All but a few thousand have a difficult time finding enough food for themselves and their families, schooling for their children, and proper medical attention. Twelve out of every one hundred babies born in Cambodia in 1989 died before their first birthdays. A major cause of these deaths was their mothers' malnutrition. Children who survived infancy were often undernourished. A U.N. study in 1984 estimated that 30 percent of Cambodia's children were underfed. Hundreds of thousands of children are orphans or have only one surviving parent. The crisis of poverty, affecting children and adults alike, makes long-term planning difficult, or impossible.

Because of insecurity and a shortage of revenue, the State of Cambodia has been unable to keep Cambodia's roads, bridges, and railway system in good repair. Trips that before 1970 took less than an hour from Phnom Penh by car, on well-paved roads, now take over three hours, on roads from which the paving has almost disappeared.

Rapid Social Change

A third theme is that for many Cambodians, as for millions of other people elsewhere in the 1990's, everything is changing so rapidly that their past experience gives little guidance for their lives. The possibility of the return of Democratic Kampuchea and the erosion of traditional values have made many Cambodians uncertain. This is particularly true for those who live abroad. People who traveled for twenty years on foot, in ox-carts, or in an occasional rickety bus now live alongside freeways where tens of thousands of cars, trucks, and buses roar past them every day. Accustomed to villages, they live in urban slums or run-down suburban areas. When they venture from home, for work or shopping, their new environment, its inhabitants, and its weather are unfamiliar, even menacing.

The freedom enjoyed by young people in the West is also distressing to many older refugees who have settled there, and so is the apparent decline of Buddhism. Cut off from their roots, many Cambodians find difficulty putting down new ones. Some have tried hard to do so, however, by becoming Christians, for example, or by working hard in high school and college.

As these changes are going on, many Cambodian immigrants have watched their children become American or French, Canadian or Australian, losing track of the past, and often losing respect for the ways that held Cambodian society together. For older Cambodians, the process has been sad to watch.

The Civil War

Finally, Cambodians in Cambodia and along the Thai border live in the shadow of an ongoing civil war. This war has sputtered along since 1980. When the Vietnamese withdrew their troops in 1989, thousands of young Cambodians were forcibly drafted into the army and trucked off to battlefronts in the northwest, while their counterparts in the refugee camps were pressed into service to fight them.

The civil war also affects civilians. Every year, hundreds of civilian men, women, and children, as well as a larger number of soldiers, have their legs or arms blown off by small plastic land mines that have been scattered throughout the country over the years by Democratic Kampuchea, the State of Cambodia, the Vietnamese, and the resistance forces. Many of the mines are undetectable until they're stepped on or touched by mistake. The pressure and the *click* that it makes on the mine activate the explosive, which blows off a hand, a foot, or more. Mines made in China and favored by Democratic Kampuchea are known as "jumping mines," because of the way they leap out of the ground when ignited.

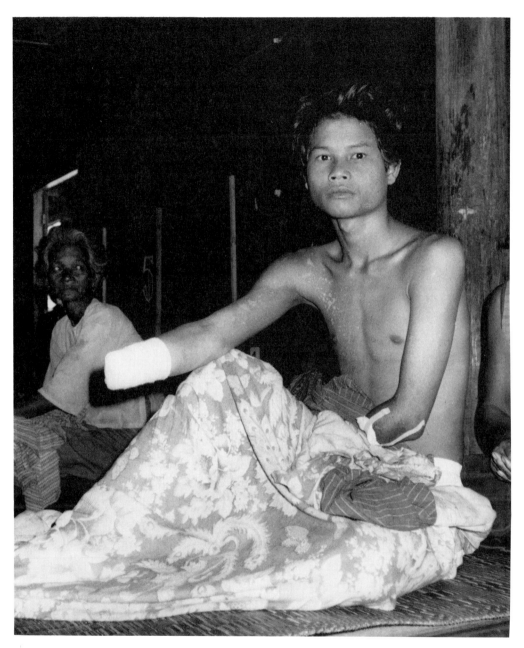

This young man, a farmer with two children, has lost both his arms due to a land mine. Thousands of Cambodian civilians have suffered from wounds like these, or worse, in the aftermath of the wars that have swept the country for twenty years.   Susan Aitken

The minefields are unmapped, and experts estimate that to clear those along the Thai border alone would require 30,000 people working for several months, during which over 10,000 of the workers would be maimed or killed.

Villagers in the late 1980's and early 1990's, especially in remote parts of the country, were also threatened by D.K. raiding parties. These ranged in size from five to a hundred men. Sometimes they offered gold for food and treated people decently, but in most cases they menaced, killed, and kidnapped rural people and tortured S.O.C. officials to death as a warning to others. Some of these D.K. fighters have been raiding villages and using their weapons against "enemies" for over twenty years.

The Sihanouk Era: A Golden Age?

The raids, the mines, the challenges of social change, and memories of Democratic Kampuchea make Cambodia different from the 1960's, a time most Cambodians over forty remember, inaccurately, as a kind of golden age.

When Sihanouk ruled Cambodia, many of his subjects believed that their lives and those of their children were secure and prosperous. This was what Sihanouk told them. Hundreds of thousands of boys and girls, many with illiterate parents, poured in and out of the nation's newly constructed schools. In Phnom Penh and provincial capitals, government clinics offered inexpensive medical care. A network of paved roads connected the country's provinces, and Cambodians were free to move around to seek employment or for pleasure. Under free-market conditions, nearly all of them had enough to eat. The war in Vietnam seemed far away.

In political terms, Sihanouk's government reacted brutally to opposition, but compared to the regimes that followed, its interference in people's daily lives was rare. With abundant exports of rice, rubber, and other crops, a high level of foreign aid, and a resilient, well-adjusted people, Cambodia seemed to be almost an enchanted country.

Appearances were deceptive. Then as now, hundreds of thousands of people had no access to clean water, schools, or medical attention. Infant mortality was higher, and annual incomes lower, than in many countries in Southeast Asia. Rice yields per acre were the lowest in the region. Rural Cambodians suffered from dysentery, tuberculosis, skin diseases, and malaria. In the cities, unemployment was high. What may have seemed like a paradise to someone passing through, looking out of a car window, was for these Cambodians a bitter struggle to survive. It was among the people in Cambodia's backwoods that the CPK gained the most recruits.

Despite these pressures in the 1960's, most people's lives moved slowly, following the rhythm of the monsoons and the agricultural year. Society was held together, it seemed, by Buddhist festivals, hierarchy, and family life. People's values included respect for the elderly, politeness, mutual assistance, and a shared feeling that life would continue along similar lines for many years.

The 1970's broke the mold. Everyone over twenty in 1990 has sharp memories of Democratic Kampuchea, and everyone over twenty-five remembers the war that preceded the Communist victory. Their experiences, their losses, the Vietnamese occupation, and pressures from outside the country have made many of them doubt earlier values and earlier patterns of behavior.

Visitors' Impressions, 1988–1989

In Phnom Penh, visitors noticed that many Cambodians had a careless, worn-down quality, as if they were speeding along a highway toward an accident they could not avoid. Observers who watched the Vietnamese

Street scene, Phnom Penh, 1989; central market in background. Between 1975 and 1979 Phnom Penh, like all Cambodian cities, was almost deserted.   Charles F. Keyes

troops leave Cambodia in September 1989 reported that their departure saddened the Cambodians looking on. They were thrown back on their own resources to fight a civil war that none of them wanted.

Others, however, approved of the Vietnamese pullout and were pleased to be owners of their land again. They began investing in the future by such gestures as roofing their houses with tile, or planting sugar palm trees, which take ten years to mature. Some, sensing the possibility of change, began studying English, paying private teachers for their lessons.

As part of its policy of opening up in 1988–1989, the State of

Children act up for the photographer, near the National Museum, Phnom Penh, 1989.   Charles F. Keyes

An eighteen-year-old mother and her newborn child, Kompong Speu hospital, 1989. Many mothers and children in Cambodia still suffer from malnutrition, and others are prone to malaria, tuberculosis, and other harsh diseases.   Susan Aitken

Cambodia invited Cambodians living abroad to visit the country. Dith Pran, the journalist whose experiences were depicted in the movie *The Killing Fields*, returned for a visit in September 1989. Pran was free to move about the country and to talk to Cambodians about the past.

He noticed the reemergence, especially in Phnom Penh, of privileged classes whose behavior reminded him of that of people in the last years of the Lon Nol regime. Most of them, as before, paid no taxes. They made their money in smuggling, speculation, and illicit trade or were high-ranking officials who benefited from overseas travel, access to large houses, and partnerships in business ventures. Bribery reemerged as a fact of life. As in the past, people's loyalties were often to family members rather than to the nation.

Everywhere he noticed sharp contrasts between what was for sale in

Phnom Penh's markets and what most Cambodians possessed. Beggars crowded into the markets, many of them young men and women without legs, or young mothers with undernourished babies. At the same time, French champagne, brought in from Singapore, sold for less in Phnom Penh than in Paris, but for more money than the beggars saw in a month. Sales of video recorders, motorcycles, and refrigerators, despite nightly curfews, poor roads, and frequent power failures, were brisk.

Nearly all government workers, who earned official salaries of less than $10 a month, took second and third jobs, or relied on bribes, working relatives, or wealthier patrons to make ends meet. Dith Pran noted during his visit: "The children of the poor become soldiers. The children of the rich become policemen [who get rich with bribes]. The children of the high cadre study in foreign countries." Another visitor, from Australia, noticed that many high school and university places were held for Party members' children and for young people orphaned under Democratic Kampuchea who had been brought up by the regime.

Many observers were fearful that pressures from Thailand, Singapore, Taiwan, and Japan on the Cambodian economy might lead to higher levels of corruption among S.O.C. officials and to a collapse of the fragile ministries built up since 1979. Some also feared the ecological side effects of uncontrolled timber-cutting, mining, and fishing. The gloomiest observers predicted that Cambodia's valuable resources, especially timber, might soon be taken away for the price it cost to bribe the appropriate officials.

Nearly all the visitors were pessimistic about the country's chances for economic recovery. This was because of the limitations placed on non-Communist aid to Cambodia by the United Nations and other bodies which refused to deal with the State of Cambodia until a political "settlement" could be reached. This boycott has isolated Cambodia from foreign investment, especially from Japan, and from foreign aid that might have assisted industry and improved communications.

Education and Cultural Activities

Although the economic outlook was bleak, visitors praised the State of Cambodia's efforts to send its people to school and to preserve traditional culture.

By the end of 1989, an estimated 1.3 million Cambodian children were enrolled at least some of the time in over 5,000 primary schools. There were also almost 300,000 secondary students in some 200 schools, and 35,000 students were enrolled in 8 colleges and universities. Over 30,000 men and women had been engaged as teachers. These raw figures compared favorably with prerevolutionary ones, and are extraordinary in view of the country's reduced resources. Conditions improved steadily through the 1980's, but even in 1989 there were severe shortages, particularly at the upper levels of the system, of textbooks, qualified teachers, laboratories, buildings, and equipment.

Much education consisted of memorizing what the teacher said. There was little effort by many teachers to relate what they taught, at the upper levels, to students' everyday experiences. At these levels many instructors taught in languages other than Khmer, such as Russian and Spanish, which were sometimes poorly understood.

On the cultural front, Indian archaeologists and their Cambodian helpers worked hard to repair war damage to the ruins of Angkor, where in some cases twenty years of vegetation had to be cleared away before restoration could begin. Visitors reported that war damage itself was slight, although many movable sculptures were missing, presumably smuggled abroad.

In Phnom Penh, the State of Cambodia supported efforts to bring

A Cambodian wedding, 1989. In recent times, the Buddhist ceremonies that had been so important in prerevolutionary Cambodia have been revived. Charles F. Keyes

Angkor Wat, January 1979. This photo was taken a week before the Communists were overthrown. The damaged statues had been placed there by Communist troops prior to being removed for safekeeping. James G. Gerrand

Cambodia's classical dance back to life. This intricate, thousand-year-old tradition, drawn originally from Indian models, has always been closely associated with the royal palace. Its dances depict scenes from Cambodian folklore and from Indian myths like the *Ramayana.* Of over two hundred trained dancers in 1975, only seventeen survived the "Pol Pot time." One of them, ironically, was Pol Pot's sister-in-law, Chea Samy, who had been a highly respected teacher since the 1940's. In the 1980's, these survivors trained new teachers and over two hundred students to become dancers in the national troupe.

The National Ballet, Phnom Penh 1989. This famous troupe, once attached to the royal palace, was devastated in the revolution, and is now reviving slowly, thanks to the survival of a few elderly teachers and government support.   Charles F. Keyes

A Cambodian comic book, 1989. A four-faced deity, probably Brahma, in a recent rendering of an ancient folktale. Comic books like these are very popular in Cambodia today. Author

Efforts were also made to revive Cambodian popular theater, folk-songs, handicrafts, painting, and other arts. The literary revival was slower. Much that was printed with P.R.K. approval in the early 1980's had a strong political message, condemning the D.K. period, emphasizing mildly socialist goals, playing down Buddhism and monarchy, and praising the friendship of Vietnam. Gradually, more traditional themes emerged, particularly in the pages of crudely printed comic books, telling tales of princes, magicians, and Angkorean times.

Economic Priorities Today

Despite these positive advances, the keys to Cambodia's security and independence, after a decade of Vietnamese occupation, were peaceful conditions and economic development. The second was impossible without the first and depended heavily, in turn, on injections of foreign money. Foreign aid after 1981 came from countries recognizing the

People's Republic of Kampuchea, the U.N. bureau UNICEF, the Red Cross, and non-governmental organizations (NGO's) from many countries. Much government-to-government aid has been focused on military items, on support for higher education, and on scholarships for Cambodian students to study overseas. Locally, funds have been used to restore Angkor, to expand education, and to maintain hospitals in Phnom Penh and the provinces.

In 1989, twenty-eight aid NGO's gave approximately $30 million in aid to the State of Cambodia. Of the 120 foreign technicians living in Cambodia, roughly one in three are medical personnel. The remainder are engineers, agricultural workers, teachers, and veterinarians.

If a settlement were reached in Cambodia that would end the civil war and bring political stability, government-to-government aid programs, as well as those financed by the United Nations, would expand enormously.

With this possibility in mind, in 1989 a team of experts selected by the United Nations studied documents provided by the State of Cambodia and other groups inside Cambodia and consulted with aid workers inside the country when they visited Bangkok so as to draw up a list of high-priority projects that its members believed could be set in motion following a political settlement.

Three urgent projects, the experts suggested, were to clear the mines from the northwestern sector of the country, to carry out a national census, and to coordinate the flow of aid into the country. High-priority projects included setting up a national agricultural documentation center, expanding factories to make farm tools, and preparing inventories of Cambodia's timber, fish, and mineral resources. Industrially, the team proposed rehabilitating Cambodia's textile mills and building up industries for processing wood and making paper.

Other proposals in the report aimed to increase Cambodia's produc-

Food stand, Phnom Penh   Charles F. Keyes

tion of electric power; to repair roads, bridges, ports, and railways; and to improve land and water transportation.

The suggestions were costly, but presumably many nations would join in financing them. They were realistic in terms of Cambodia's urgent needs, its resources, and its capabilities. The sooner the proposals, or others like them, could be set in motion, the better it would be for Cambodia's long-suffering people.

Already, since 1979, Cambodian men and women have taken heroic strides on their own, and with limited assistance, to bring their country back from the brink of annihilation. They have constantly had to struggle with political considerations. Some of these involve Cambodian leaders anxious to repeat the errors of the past and willing to kill their fellow countrymen to gain their ends. Others involve foreigners, who claim that Cambodia is not important, or who claim to know what is best for Cambodians. After so many false promises, and so much pain, the time had come, at the end of the 1980's, for the ancient country of Cambodia to rejoin the world. Doing so would allow its people to continue along the path they have followed, with so many ups and downs, for over two thousand years.

Bibliography

Books and Articles

Two excellent bibliographies on Cambodia are Charles F. Keyes, *Southeast Asian Research Tools: Cambodia* (Honolulu: University of Hawaii Press, 1979) and John Marston, *An Annotated Bibliography of Cambodia and Cambodian Refugees* (Minneapolis: Center for Urban and Regional Affairs, University of Minnesota, 1987).

Chapter I

There are many firsthand accounts of the evacuation of Phnom Penh. The best ones are probably those by the French missionary François Ponchaud, *Cambodia Year Zero* (New York: Holt, Rinehart & Winston, 1978); the former student Someth May, *Cambodian Witness* (New York: Random House, 1986); and Molyda Szymusiak, *The Stones Cry Out* (New York: Hill & Wang, 1986), the story of the experiences of a Cambodian girl who was ten years old in 1975.

Chapter II

For a readable introduction to Cambodia's land and people in prerevolutionary times, see T. J. Abercrombie's "Cambodian Life and Culture: Indochina's 'Neutral Corner' " *National Geographic,* Vol. 126, pp. 614–61 (October 1964). Younger readers might consult Ruth Tooze, *Cambodia: Land of Contrasts* (New York: Viking, 1962). For more detail, see Donald Whitaker, *Area Handbook for the Khmer Republic (Cambodia)* (Washington: U.S. Government Printing Office, 1974). A more recent, readable study is the Lutheran Immigration and Refugee Service's *Cambodia: The Land and Its People* (New York: Lutheran Council in the USA, 1983), which includes data about Cambodian refugees in the United States.

Chapter III

Little anthropological work exists on Cambodia in English. May Ebihara, *Svay, A Khmer Village in Cambodia* (Ann Arbor, MI: University Microfilms, 1971) is an outstanding study based on fieldwork in a village near Phnom Penh in 1959–1960. See also Ebihara's helpful essay "Khmer Village Women in Cambodia: A Happy Balance" in Carolyn J. Matthiasson (ed.), *Many Sisters* (New York: Free Press, 1974, pp. 305–47).

Chapter IV

For short accounts of Cambodia's early history, see David P. Chandler, *A History of Cambodia* (Boulder, CO: Westview Press, 1983), chapter 2, and Charles Higham's useful study *The Archaeology of Mainland Southeast Asia* (Cambridge, UK: Cambridge University Press, 1988), chapters 4 and 5. See also Donn Bayard, "The Roots of Indo-Chinese Civilization: Recent Developments in the Pre-History of Southeast Asia," *Pacific Affairs,* vol. 53 pp. 89–114 (Spring 1980), and Jean Boisselier, *Trends in Khmer Art* (Ithaca, NY: Cornell University Southeast Asia Program, 1989)—an excellent, readable study.

Chapter V

There are many valuable books about Angkor. One of the best, and shortest, is G. Coedès, *Angkor: An Introduction* (New York: Oxford University Press, 1963). See also Christopher Pym's readable treatment *The Ancient Civilization of Angkor* (New

York: Mentor, 1968). For a thirteenth-century eyewitness account, see Chou Ta Kuan, *The Customs of Cambodia* (ed. J. G. Paul; Bangkok: 1987). More recent visits are described in W. Robert Moore, "Angkor: Jewel of the Jungle," *National Geographic* Vol. 117, pp. 516–69 (April 1960), and Peter White, "The Temples of Angkor: Ancient Glory in Stone," *National Geographic* Vol. 161, pp. 552–89 (May 1982). On the conditions of the temples in 1989, see Russell L. Ciochon, "Jungle Monuments of Angkor," *Natural History,* pp. 52–59 (January 1990). Younger readers might enjoy I. G. Edmunds, *The Khmers of Cambodia: The Story of a Mysterious People* (New York: Bobbs-Merrill, 1970).

Chapter VI

Cambodia's history between the fall of Angkor and the arrival of the French has not received much attention in English-language sources. See David P. Chandler, *A History of Cambodia,* chapters 5, 6, and 7. On the rediscovery of Angkor in 1860 see Henri Mouhot, *Henri Mouhot's Diary* (ed. C. Pym; Kuala Lumpur: Oxford University Press, 1966). There are no detailed studies of Cambodian literature in English. For some Cambodian folktales, see David P. Chandler (tr.), *Favorite Stories from Cambodia* (Exeter, NH dist.: Heinemann in Asia, 1978), and Jewell R. Coburn (tr.), *Khmers, Tigers and Talismans* (Thousand Oaks, CA: Burn, Hart and Co., 1978).

Chapter VII

The best study of the early colonial period in English is Milton Osborne, *Rule and Response* (Ithaca, NY: Cornell University Press, 1969). See also Osborne's stimulating book about the Mekong River exploration, *River Road to China* (New York: Liveright, 1975). For the remainder of the colonial period, see David P. Chandler, *A History of Cambodia,* chapters 8 and 9.

Chapter VIII

The Sihanouk period is treated perceptively in two books by Milton Osborne: *Power and Politics in Cambodia* (Hawthorn, Australia: Longmans, 1973) and *Before Kampuchea* (Sydney and London: Allen & Unwin, 1979), a memoir of Osborne's time in Cambodia in the 1960's. See also Roger M. Smith, *Cambodia's Foreign Policy* (Ithaca, NY: Cornell University Press, 1965) and John Armstrong, *Sihanouk Speaks* (New York: Walter and Company, 1964), an admiring account, based on interviews.

Unfortunately, Sihanouk's memoirs, written in French, have not yet been translated into English.

The best book about the Lon Nol period is William Shawcross, *Sideshow: Nixon, Kissinger and the Destruction of Cambodia* (New York: Simon & Schuster, 1979), a devastating critique of U.S. policy. See also Norodom Sihanouk with Wilfred Burchett, *My War with the CIA* (New York: Pantheon, 1972), a less judicious attack; and Arnold Isaacs's comprehensive *Without Honor: Defeat in Vietnam and Cambodia* (Baltimore: Johns Hopkins University Press, 1983, pp. 188–292).

For an interesting analysis of the rise of Communism in Cambodia before 1975, see Ben Kiernan, *How Pol Pot Came to Power* (New York: Schocken, 1985). Some of the same ground is covered in Elizabeth Becker, *When the War Was Over* (New York: Simon & Schuster, 1986). For a valuable collection of essays and documents about radicalism in Cambodia, generally sympathetic to the radical cause but opposed to Pol Pot's brand of Communism, see Ben Kiernan and Chantou Boua, *Peasants and Politics in Kampuchea, 1942–1982* (Armonk, NY: M. J. Sharpe, 1983).

Chapter IX

In addition to the books mentioned for chapter 1, see Craig Etcheson's useful summary *The Rise and Demise of Democratic Kampuchea* (Boulder, CO: Westview Press, 1985); and Michael Vickery's more controversial (and more penetrating) analysis *Cambodia 1975–1982* (Boston: South End Press, 1983). Sydney Schanberg, *The Death and Life of Dith Pran* (New York: Viking Penguin, 1985) is a useful study that formed the basis of the movie *The Killing Fields*. See also Haing Ngor, *A Cambodian Odyssey* (New York: Macmillan, 1987). Haing Ngor won an Oscar for his portrayal of Dith Pran in *The Killing Fields. A Cambodian Odyssey* describes his own experiences under Pol Pot and afterward.

Several collections of essays cover aspects of revolutionary Cambodia. These include David P. Chandler and Ben Kiernan (eds.), *Revolution and Its Aftermath in Kampuchea* (New Haven, CT: Yale University Southeast Asia Program, 1983); David P. Chandler, Ben Kiernan, and Chantou Boua (ed. and tr.), *Pol Pot Plans the Future: Confidential Leadership Documents from Democratic Kampuchea, 1976–1977* (New Haven, CT: Yale University Southeast Asia Program, 1988); and Karl Jackson (ed.), *Cambodia 1975–1978: Rendez-vous with Death* (Princeton, NJ: Princeton University Press, 1989). Jackson's book contains helpful analyses of the Pol Pot era by U.S. government officials and others.

A gripping tale of how one upper-class family struggles against the terrors of the Red Khmer in the late 1970's before at last escaping to America is found in *To Destroy You Is No Loss: The Odyssey of a Cambodian Family* by Joan V. Criddle and Teeda Butt Man (New York: Atlantic Monthly, 1987).

Cambodian Witness: The Autobiography of Someth May (New York: Random House, 1986) gives the reader a "behind-the-scenes" look at the horrors of the "killing fields"—from one who survived, but only while watching the deaths of many friends and loved ones.

A judicious analysis of the 1970's is Kimmo Kiljunen's *Kampuchea: Decade of the Genocide.* (London: Zed Books, 1984).

Chapter X

The most thorough study of Cambodia since 1979 is Michael Vickery, *Kampuchea: Politics, Economics and Society* (Boulder, CO: Lin Reinner, 1987); it is sympathetic to the P.R.K. regime. On Cambodia's war with Vietnam, see Nayan Chanda, *Brother Enemy* (New York: Harcourt, 1986), by a veteran correspondent, and the somewhat more analytical study by two Australian scholars, Grant Evans and Kelvin Rowley, *Red Brotherhood at War* (London: Vista, 1984, rev. ed. 1990). William Shawcross, *The Quality of Mercy* (New York: Simon & Schuster, 1986) analyzes the international response to the Cambodian crisis in 1979–1982. The same confusing period is treated in Norodom Sihanouk, *War and Hope: The Case for Cambodia* (New York: Pantheon, 1980), written before Sihanouk joined in a coalition "government" with the Communists. See also John Pilger and Anthony Barnett, *Aftermath: The Struggle of Cambodia and Vietnam* (London: New Statesman, 1981); and David A. Ablin and Marlowe Hood (eds.), *The Cambodian Agony* (Armonk, NY: M. E. Sharpe, 1987).

A good, recent account of how a Cambodian refugee struggles to "fit in" at her high school is Linda Crew's *Children of the River* (New York: Delacorte Press, 1989).

Chapter XI

The best pictorial account of Cambodia today is unfortunately somewhat out of date: Peter White, "Kampuchea Awakens from a Nightmare," *National Geographic* Vol.

161, pp. 590–622 (May 1982). Major U.S. newspapers such as *The New York Times,* the *Washington Post,* and the *Los Angeles Times,* available in microform, contain a good deal of coverage of local conditions, and the journal *Asian Survey* each year publishes essays on the preceding year's developments in Cambodia and other Asian countries. Authors of recent Cambodian articles include Elizabeth Becker, Nayan Chanda, Timothy Carney, and Karl D. Jackson. Similar surveys also appear annually in the review *Southeast Asian Affairs*, published by the Institute of Southeast Asian Affairs in Singapore, and roughly every other year in the journal *Current History.*

Filmography

The most important movie dealing with Cambodia is undoubtedly David Putnam's *The Killing Fields,* produced in 1984.

Discography

Music of Cambodia. The Sam-ang Ensemble (World Music Institute: WHI 007). *Traditional Music of Cambodia.* Available from Center for the Study of Khmer Culture, 27 Knowles Avenue, Middletown, CT 06457. Cassettes of modern Cambodian music are obtainable from specialty shops in cities with sizeable refugee populations, such as Long Beach, CA; Seattle-Tacoma, WA; Washington, DC; and Dallas, TX, among others.

Index

Numbers in *italics* refer to illustrations.

ABOUT THE AUTHOR

David P. Chandler is Research Director of Southeast
Asian Studies at Monash University in Melbourne, Australia. He is the author of a number of books on Cambodia, including a forthcoming biography of Pol Pot.